AF322725

Pardon Me, My Ontology Is Showing

Realizing You're Already on the Porch (Even if You Brought Your Legal Briefs)

Angie Day Peters

PARDON ME, MY ONTOLOGY IS SHOWING *Realizing You're Already on the Porch (Even If You Brought Your Legal Briefs)*

Copyright © 2026 by Angie Day Peters

Published by MV Press, an imprint of Mavyn Vue, LLC.

www.mavynvue.com

ISBN: 979-8-234-05123-3 (Hardback)

Library of Congress Control Number: 2026909007

Cover Design and Illustration: Angie Day Peters

Interior Layout: Angie Day Peters

Unless otherwise indicated, Scripture quotations are from the Holy Bible, New International Version®, NIV®. Copyright © 1973, 1978, 1984, 2011 by Biblica, Inc.™ Used by permission of Zondervan. All rights reserved worldwide.

Printed in the United States of America First Edition: May 2026

DEDICATION

To John.

You were the wanderer, and I was the one white-knuckling the rules—two different prodigals lost in the same house. I am so grateful for the Father who held steady, unmoved by our roles, and simply called us home.

In the seasons that felt like an unending dark night, you were the reprieve of the Savior to me. You never tired of the battle; you simply secured me in an embrace where the distance dissolved and the love of Jesus became my reality. You loved me until the light came up.

I love who you are.

CONTENTS

PREFACE

The Architecture of the Ache

I am staring down the barrel of fifty, and I have spent nearly half a century serving as the lead paralegal in the ongoing case against my own soul.

I was a professional at the litigation of Not Enough. I didn't just show up to the courtroom; I arrived early with color-coded binders, a perfectly pressed tea-length dress, and enough 'Legal Briefs' to bury a small city. I had a file for every failure, a memo for every 'ought-to', and a spreadsheet for my spiritual progress that would make a Pharisee weep with envy. I even brought the 1950s housewife smile—that high-gloss, fragile veneer—to mask the fact that my Ontology was, frankly, a mess.

We call this living, but for most of us, it's just a perpetual audit.

We walk into the rooms of our lives—our kitchens, our office cubicles, our church foyers—with a metaphorical clipboard in hand. We are constantly checking the vents for dust and our hearts for any sign of unapproved joy. We think that if we can just justify our existence through enough effort, we can finally rest. I spent decades building an architecture out of my aches, convinced that if I designed the structure perfectly, kept the floors polished, and the rules white-knuckled, the Father would finally feel comfortable enough to visit.

I thought God lived in the case for the defense. I thought He was the Judge waiting for me to finish my closing argument.

But in the middle of all that polished performance, I started to hear something. It wasn't a shout, and it certainly wasn't a new set of instructions. A low, steady, and impossibly calm whistle sounded. It was coming from the Porch. While I was busy litigating my own unworthiness, the Father was just whistling. It was the sound of someone who had already settled the case while I was still obsessing over the briefs.

That sound is the holy scandal I discovered while I was busy filing my latest grievance: The audit is a lie. The courtroom is an empty theater, and the floorboards we've been pacing on are incredibly thin.

And the woman on the cover? She isn't just having a moment of artistic flair. The performance is reaching its breaking point for her. The trial she has been winning—or losing—was settled before she was even born. She isn't just throwing papers; she's throwing away the entire trial.

This is not a book about how to fix your life. That would just be me handing you a new set of binders and a better clipboard. This is a book about what happens when you realize you were never the defendant, the prosecution has dismissed the case, and you already own the Porch.

The door isn't just unlocked; it was removed from its hinges a long time ago.

So, pardon me. my Ontology is showing. I'm dropping the briefs, I'm leaving the courtroom, and I'm going to go sit in the sun. I think you should come, too.

PART I
THE COURTROOM OF MAN

The floorboards of the audit are loud, but they are thin. Before we step into the trial, remember: we aren't here to win a case, but to realize the Judge has already left the building to walk us home.

1

The Barabbas Paradox

THE MOB ROARED. IT WAS A CHAOTIC, HEAVING mass of humanity, its collective breath a hot, desperate prayer for a specific fairness. They wanted a version of justice they could understand—one that calculated the debt of their oppressors and demanded a payment in blood. On the stone platform stood two men, an impossible study in contrasts. One was Jesus of Nazareth, the self-proclaimed Son of Man, a man of profound peace and quiet authority, whose hands had healed the sick. The other was the insurrectionist, a notorious rebel whose hands had shed blood in a frantic attempt to balance the world's accounts.

Both men stood as mirrors of the crowd's internal struggle. The people longed for the one whose embrace could satisfy their anguish, but an internal delusion drove them toward a warrior who promised to make things right through force. To the crowd, the choice seemed simple. In Pilate's view, it was a political maneuver. To Heaven, it was the moment of truth.

Which one do you want me to release to you? Pilate asked, his voice cutting through the din.

This was no ordinary choice between an innocent man and a criminal. This was a public and definitive referendum on the nature of God's heart. As the demand for the rebel rose, the air seemed to thicken with that stale, ancient dust. It was the smell of a people so accustomed to the damp basement of getting what you deserve that the restoration offered by the Son felt like a threat to their very lungs.

They reached for the familiar rot of the transactional system because it was predictable. In our Western minds, we have amplified the concept of equal-pay-for-equal-pain to the nth degree. We find a strange security in the audit, preferring a God who keeps a ledger to a Father who offers a feast. The musty scent of the status quo felt safer than the wild, uncontained River that Jesus was offering.

The Dichotomy of the Swords: Retribution versus Restoration

THE CROWD'S DESPERATE CRY WAS NOT A SIMPLE WHIM; it was a foundational statement about the kind of Messiah—and the kind of justice—humanity was conditioned to demand. At that moment, the world stood at a crossroads, forced to choose between two antithetical powers: Retributive Justice, which operates by the math of the debt, and Restorative Justice, which operates by the flow of Reconciliation.

The people chose the counting house, believing the only

path to freedom was through vengeance and payment. They chose a justice that looks backward at the crime, rather than a justice that looks forward toward the original intent. We know this system intimately; it is the eye for an eye economy. Its focus is the past and the resulting deficit. Its goal is to punish the wrongdoer and inflict proportional pain to satisfy the offended party or the broken law.

The outcome of this system is always condemnation, isolation, and a debt that can never be fully settled. It is a cold, clinical weight that leaves the soul empty—smelling of that same musty stagnation I felt in the jury box. This is the courtroom theology, in which God acts as a Judge requiring strict legal satisfaction. It suggests a life of constant emotional accounting —the lie that if you wander; you have created a deficit in God's heart that only a payment can fill. But the Father is not a bookkeeper; He is a Presence. He doesn't see a debt to be collected; He sees a child to be gathered.

But the Father is not a bookkeeper; He doesn't keep records of wrongs. He is like a master architect holding a plumb line against a leaning wall; He isn't weighing the bricks to find their fault; He is singing them back into alignment.

The Strategy of the Turned Cheek

To understand the River, we must look at the radical commands Jesus gave in the Sermon on the Mount. We often read the instruction to turn the other cheek or give your coat as a call to passive doormat-theology. But in the audit's context, these were revolutionary acts of de-escalation and systemic refusal. They were a way to blow fresh, oxygenated air into a room that had been sealed shut by the dusty history of retribution.

When Jesus said, *You have heard that it was said, 'An eye for an eye and a tooth for a tooth.' But I say to you, Do not resist the one who is evil* (Matthew 5:38-39), He was directly addressing the Law of Retribution. The eye for an eye is the ultimate mantra of the transactional life. The principle seeks to prevent global chaos by ensuring punishments do not exceed crimes, but it inherently traps everyone in a debt cycle. If you take my eye, the only way I can feel just is to take yours. Now we are both blind, and the debt is settled but the air is still stagnant and stale; no one is healed.

Jesus's alternative—turning the cheek, offering the cloak, walking the extra mile—is the active practice of the River.

Turning the Cheek: This is a refusal to join the transactional dance of the blow. By not striking back, you refuse to validate the math of the exchange. You stop the musty momentum of the eye for an eye in its tracks.

Offering the Coat: When the Law demands your shirt,

Jesus says to give your cloak as well. This is a move of aggressive generosity. It shatters the transactional nature of the lawsuit by giving more than what is owed. It moves the interaction from a stale courtroom of debt to a porch of abundance.

This is the groundwork of Restorative Justice: the realization that the only way to defeat a system of debt is to introduce a currency the system doesn't recognize—Grace. When you turn the cheek, you aren't being weak; you are being sovereign. You declare that the person who struck you do not manage your identity. You are choosing to stay in the current, where the flow of God's life is more powerful than the demand for vengeance.

Jesus, the Reconciling King, refused to engage in the audit. He did not ask what payment was due; He asked what wholeness was possible. His justice was not a debt that needed to be satisfied, but a powerful, living force meant to heal broken relationships, reconcile enemies, and bring all things back into harmony with God.

The Sword and the Bandit

THE PEOPLE, DROWNING IN A CULTURE OF RETRIBUTION, could not conceive of a Messiah who would conquer not with a sword that inflicts pain, but with a love that absorbs it. They chose the familiar, musty logic of vengeance over the terrifying freedom of the River.

The first-century world experienced widespread messianic expectations. Ancient promises, specifically prophecies depicting a majestic king who would bring triumph and restoration, formed the basis of the people's anticipation for a coming deliverer. But their perspective had become stale, filtered through the damp walls of Roman oppression. These biblical texts created the hope for a kingly messiah, a political warrior from the line of David who would liberate Israel through the only justice they understood: the sword.

God's promise to David, *I will raise up your offspring...and I will establish his kingdom forever* (2 Samuel 7:12-13), fueled this longing for an eternal, conquering ruler. The prophet Isaiah spoke of a child whose government would rest on his shoulders, one who would *uphold it with justice and with righteousness* (Isaiah 9:6-7). The people interpreted these promises through the stagnant lens of a forceful political takeover.

The hope for a political messiah was not a vague dream; it was a tangible reality found in men like Barabbas, the insurrectionist. Historical context from Jewish historians tells us that the term used to describe him, bandit (*lestes*), was often a Roman term for a political rebel or guerrilla fighter. He was more than a common criminal; he was a leader in a violent insurrection, a man who had not only defied Rome but had done so with bloodshed. He was the living embodiment of the sword they longed for—the very messiah they believed their prophecies had promised.

But Jesus was not just a contradiction to this vision; He was a profound redefinition of it. He refused to be a political king, proclaiming His kingdom was not of this world and rebuking Peter for drawing a sword in His defense. He was the fresh air in a room full of ancient, heavy smoke. He was not a king who needed an earthly throne to reign, a priest who needed a temple to offer sacrifice, or a prophet who needed a scroll to speak His word. He was the divine Son of God who perfectly fulfilled and utterly transcended every messianic hope.

The prisoner walking free that day—the man who didn't ask for his life, who didn't petition the court, and who didn't offer a single act of penance—is the physical proof of the ancient promise in Isaiah 61—the one that declares a year where every debt is cancelled and every prison door is swung wide, not by merit, but by royal decree. He is the prototype of the unearned exhale. He was the first to experience the *Year of the Lord's Favor* while the crowd was still arguing over the *Day of Vengeance*. He walked away not because he had balanced the scales, but because the King had already decided that the prisoner was worth more than the crime.

The Jury Box and the Kitchen Knife

THERE IS SOMETHING ABOUT A COURTHOUSE THAT evokes guilt. As I walked up the old staircase, every creak of the wood seemed to amplify the fear already resounding inside of me, as if the very building were accusing me of a secret I didn't know I kept. The atmosphere was thick and musty, a vibe that felt like a silent verdict had already been rendered. I could feel an old friend, my perfectionism, attempting to creep up inside of me—an insulation and covering I knew all too well. The older brother, my internal auditor, conditioned to perform and hide, immediately took notice of the room's weight.

Inside the courtroom, I sat in the jury box, awaiting the judge's appearance. She walked in, robed in authority and wearing the Judicial black. I recognized the power of the position, but felt an internal conviction: I was not here to be a judge over measures, but over love's ambition. I did not hold a gavel in my hand, but promise and hope. When I looked at the man accused of the crime—a murder for insurance money—I could sense his fear, perhaps the hope of innocence I detected. His life was on the line, and he was terrified. From my seat in the box, I could see his face clearly. I watched as he nervously repositioned his body over and over, his restlessness a physical manifestation of the audit we were all subjected to in that room. It was a mirror of my own internal fidgeting. I realized I was sitting at a crossroads of two different courtrooms: the one in that room, which demanded a sword to settle the score, and the one in my heart, where the Father was inviting me to leave the platform entirely. I wasn't just watching a trial; I was watching the Barabbas choice play out in real-time, right in front of me.

The Anatomy of a Breach

Amid hearing the evidence, the conversation I was having with the Holy Spirit centered on my own heartache. We discovered that a family member groomed our daughters, a betrayal of the most sacred trust that felt as if the sun itself had extinguished.

The irony was a jagged pill. Only a week before the floor fell out, this individual—a twenty-nine-year-old cousin we loved and trusted—had sat in our living room on a Sunday evening. This is after a Sunday morning service where the message was a powerful account of God's relentless love for everyone. He provoked a conversation, clearly wrestling—not only with a theological idea, but with his own soul. He flatly asked, "Do you believe God's grace covers everything? No matter what it is?" My husband and I leaned in. We saw his tears, and we felt a holy obligation to prove the truth of God's nature to him. As practitioners of the 'Finished Work,' we wanted him to know we included him. 'You don't know what I've done!' he admitted. We didn't care; we told him the debt was settled.

We offered him the very peace he was currently using as a cloak for his crimes. To later grapple with the fact that we had championed the inclusion of the man who was destroying our children was a crisis of faith that left us questioning if we had been fools for the Gospel. Yet, in the years of sifting that followed, we reached a terrifying, holy conclusion: Though we struggled with the timing, we cannot deny that what we told him that night was the absolute truth of the Gospel. The 'Finished Work' didn't stop being finished because he had been predatory. The truth of God's nature remained steady even when our own world was being dismantled. We realized that while his actions were a systemic theft; they didn't have the power to un-write the Word we had spoken over him. Grace didn't become a lie just because it was hard to hold.

In hindsight, we knew the full extent of the darkness. This wasn't a singular fracture; it was a systemic theft of the most sacred kind. We were looking at a man who had allowed a predatory lie to consume his nature—one who was methodically reaching for the futures of three of our own daughters. But the depth of the betrayal didn't stop at our door. It was only as we sat in the wreckage of our own despair that a horrific pattern emerged. I looked at the life of our niece, watching the way her world had inexplicably fallen apart years prior, and the realization hit me with the force of a physical blow. I knew. When asked, she confirmed: he had already claimed her innocence, too.

The acts were unspeakable—acts of pedophilia and sexual violence that leave a permanent weight on the soul of a mother. But the true terror of a breach like this is the way the truth leaks out in slow, jagged installments. A few years after the initial nightmare began, the sharpest detail finally surfaced, a detail that had been hidden behind a wall of fear: the night he had trapped our oldest daughter on the kitchen countertop, the cold steel of a kitchen knife pulled to ensure her silence. We stood in the aftermath of a total system failure.

The Expiration of the Audit

WE HAD BEEN THROUGH HELL RECOVERING FROM IT ALL. It was a nightmare that lived in our bones. We had sought legal action, desperately hoping the system of the world would offer the protection it promised, but the evidence was a ghost we couldn't catch. Though legality was all we knew, we didn't want to put our daughters through the additional trauma of a legal system that demanded they perform their pain for a verdict.

We retreated into our grief, feeling as though the world's

version of justice had abandoned us. What was fascinating was that on this particular day, sitting in that jury box years later, the statute of limitations had ended for us to take legal action in our own case. I sat there, stunned by the realization of it. The ten-year window expired that very month—perhaps even that very day. It felt as if God had orchestrated my presence in this jury box for my own sake, pulling me into the room where the world's justice lives just to show me its boundaries.

The window was slamming shut, but as I sat there, I realized I wasn't reaching for the handle. I wasn't seeking legality. I didn't want a verdict that would only balance a ledger; I was looking for a restoration that would heal a lineage. A world-system's extraction of a pound of flesh wasn't needed to make me feel 'even.' A Father-Reality was needed to restore what was stolen. I wasn't looking for a balanced ledger; I was looking for a healed lineage. The window of legality slammed shut, and for the first time, I realized I didn't need the courthouse keys because I was already standing in the open air of the Porch. The ability for the world to extract its demanded satisfaction was gone, and to my surprise, I was okay with letting the window close. This proved that true justice defies confinement to a timeframe or a legal statute. The courtroom may have run out of time, but the river was still flowing, carrying a freshness that those musty halls could never contain.

The Liturgy of the Not Ready

IN THAT SEASON—THE ONE WHERE THE WINDOW WAS still open and the pain was fresh—I was a stranger to the language of the 'exhale.' I lived in a state of high-alert, fueled by a fury that felt more honest than any prayer I could muster. While everyone around us seemed to prefer that I simply 'get over it'—as if a polite distance could cure a systemic violation —I was screaming.

My liturgy was the Dixie Chicks' anthem, *Not Ready to Make Nice*. I leaned into the defiance of that song as if it were a shield. I wasn't interested in the cheap, religious version of forgiveness that demands a forgetful mind while the heart is still hemorrhaging. I wasn't being difficult; I was being truthful. When the world—and especially the church—pressured me to back down for the sake of an artificial peace, I sang back with that same fierce refusal to go 'round and 'round' with a lie. I couldn't do what everyone thought I should, because to make nice was to agree with the delusion that the theft didn't matter. I was standing on the stone platform of retribution, and the only thing that felt just was the heat of my own anger.

The Deliberation

EVENTUALLY, THE ROAR OF THE ANTHEM FADES. THE FAmiliar heat gives way to the heavy, collective stillness of the jury box. As I sat there, I was aware of the space directly behind me —the row where the family of the murdered woman sat. They were doing their best to hold the line of their own composure, but I could feel the tremor of their hearts through the very air. In that room, two different kinds of silence were colliding: the clinical, low-voltage hum of the law and the thick, suffocating silence of a grief that has no vocabulary. It was the crushing, stagnant weight of deciding a man's fate under the rules of the audit. They released us to deliberate on the afternoon of the second day. To my surprise, the room was divided, hung up on proper evidence. The conversations fascinated me; voices were laced with frustration and anger, needing not just to be right but agreed with. I observed for the first couple of hours, yet a powerful pull compelled me to speak and be heard. I cannot recall my words, but I know peace flowed from me like a gentle river. The next vote all had shifted but one.

The Uniform of the Audit

WE WOULD SPEND THE NEXT DAY AND A HALF ATTEMPTing to convince a dear woman who seemed overcome by the bondage of her own religion. I watched her over those three days, and her presence was a study in unyielding boundaries. She was a woman of small stature, always seated in a heavy denim skirt that reached down to her ankles—a fabric that didn't just cover, but seemed to anchor her to a specific set of rules. She wore a long-sleeved top that she buttoned up neatly. She pulled her hair back tightly into a bun that was so precise and so firm; it looked like a physical knot of her own resolve. She wore her theology like a silhouette.

The issue for her was not about the evidence at hand; she decidedly declared the defendant's guilt. But she refused to side with the prosecutor. The prosecutor was a woman in a position of authority, whereas the defendant's lawyer was an older, curious man who didn't seem to put much effort into his case. However, we could not sway the woman in the denim skirt.

It was about the right and wrong ingrained in her from childhood. In her world, women could not hold power. It was deeply ironic: a woman had been brutally murdered, and yet, religion could approve of her death before the conviction of the murderer. This woman's internal accounting was so heavily weighted by religious rule and gender-based legalism that it obscured the simple, ethical demand for a decisive vote. The spirit of religious legalism, obsessed with internal order and compliance, had become a greater authority than the pursuit of truth. She sat there, a prisoner of her own good label, choosing the safety of the knot over the freedom of the verdict.

Measureless Justice

Right there in that courtroom, God was having a conversation with me about justice. He would ask me what I knew, and if I understood the implications of leaving justice in the hands of the world. I realized that when we do not understand His justice, we default to the justice system of the world, and it holds us to those dictates. However, if we understand God's justice and pronounce that over our lives, the systems of the world have no hold on us. God's justice is not about measures at all. It's about redemption, hope, and living life to the fullest. His justice looks at the full scope of a life and decides which path leads to truth. A woman had said to me, with a tone of arrogance, as I was leaving for the first day of court, "The Lord wants to teach you something about Justice!". I knew what her aim was; she had hoped God would refine my political sensibility—the justice that cries out for Barabbas. I certainly learned something unexpected about justice, but not as she supposed.

The Choice of the Messiah

Commentators often interpret the Barabbas exchange story as a simple choice between a criminal and an innocent man, but it was far more profound. The crowd was offered a choice between two kings, two versions of a Messiah, and two entirely different approaches to justice.

On one side was the revolutionary. He used violence and insurrection to fight for an earthly kingdom and for a people who longed to be free from Rome's oppression. The justice he represented was retributive—an "Eye for an Eye," punishment for a crime, and liberation through the sword of war. He was the hero of the musty basement, the one who promised to balance the accounts through the familiar weight of vengeance. When the crowd cried out for him, they were choosing a specific justice that aligned with their desire to see someone pay.

On the other side stood Jesus, the King of the Jews. The justice He embodied was restorative—a powerful, living force meant to heal broken relationships, reconcile enemies, and bring all things back into harmony with God. It wasn't a justice that sought to make things pay, but one that sought to make things whole. This is the river of reconciliation—not a flash flood of judgment, but a life-giving current of God's redemptive love that washes away the stagnant scent of our failure.

The choice between them was a choice between two antithetical powers. The rebel relied on a cold, external sword of violence to balance the scales. Jesus did not merely carry a message; He is the Word made flesh. The Living Word doesn't strike to wound; it shines to reveal. This 'sword' is the surgical light of His Countenance, gently separating the 'Adam' from your true identity. He isn't cutting away 'bad parts' to satisfy a standard; He is peeling back the suffocating layers of a lie so the real you can finally breathe the oxygen of the Porch. The insurrectionist's sword cuts down the enemy to satisfy a debt; Jesus, as the Living Word, acts as a surgical instrument of redefinition.

He does not punish the guilty self, but separates the truth from the lie (Hebrews 4:12). Where the world's sword destroys the person to settle the score, the Living Word cuts away the lie of attainment without damaging the identity of the child. His Presence proclaims our secured identity, cutting through the layers of shame and performance anxiety that bind us, and revealing the holy, loved being beneath the striving. It is a sword used for restoration, not retribution.

A Different Justice

To fully grasp the magnitude of this shift, we must look at how Jesus lived. His ministry was a series of acts that proved a different justice was at hand—a justice that carries the scent of a fresh sea breeze rather than the stale, recycled air of a courthouse.

Consider the moment the collectors cornered Peter for the temple tax. The world's system had placed a 'demand' on his head—a clinical, cold requirement to prove he belonged. At that moment, Peter wasn't just facing a bill; he was facing the Audit.

But look at the Father's response to Jesus. He didn't give Peter a lecture on financial responsibility or a 'loan' he'd have to repay. He did not even acknowledge the 'legitimacy' of the debt. He simply pointed to the abundance of the Father's world. 'Go to the sea,' He said.

When Peter found that coin in the fish's mouth, it wasn't a 'legal settlement.' It was a royal provision. The Father wasn't 'satisfying a debt' for Peter; He demonstrated His children live from a Source that the counting house cannot comprehend. He pulled the answer out of the water to show that His goodness is always a landslide ahead of any 'requirement' the world can dream up. He didn't just pay a tax; He protected a son.

We see this same pattern earlier in Peter's life. After a long, fruitless night of fishing, Peter and his companions had nothing to show for their labor. Their nets were empty; their work, a failure. In a world of clinical scarcity and condemnation, this failure would lead to shame and a lack of provision.

But Jesus steps into the moment not to punish the lack of results, but to reverse it. He tells them to let their nets down for a catch, and when they do, they fill the nets to the point of breaking. Jesus did not simply provide a catch; He restored what was lost and provided an abundance that went beyond their greatest efforts.

These stories of the miraculous coin and the overflowing nets were prophetic signs. They showed that His justice was not a punishment for what we lack, but a provision for all that we need. He is singing us back to the plumb line of our original design.

The Echo of the Choice

HISTORY ECHOES THE CHOICE MADE ON THAT STONE platform outside Jerusalem because we must make it daily. The mob, in its exhausted craving for vengeance, chose a king who validated its rage and demanded equivalent payment. They chose the familiar, reliable mechanism of the audit—the same breathless system I felt closing in on me in the jury box.

But the Father was offering a terrifying freedom: the river of reconciliation that required no payment. He offered the complete dissolution of the debt, not merely a transfer of its weight.

The genuine tragedy of this paradox is that we often stand in the crowd, having already received the freedom Christ offered, and yet we still raise our voices for the criminal. We shout for the rebel every time we default to self-condemnation, spiritual pride, or fear of God's auditing eye. We are choosing the king who uses the sword of violence—even if that violence is spiritual, directed inward, and aimed at the hollow lie of attainment that tells us we aren't yet enough.

We are choosing a justice that seeks to make us pay, over a King who sought only to make us whole.

The echo of that choice reverberates in our hearts every time we cling to the counting house, believing we must achieve balance through punishment. But the river flows with a different song—a song of freedom, of reconciliation, of wholeness. It invites us to step out of the crowd, to lay down the sword of self-condemnation, and to embrace the terrifying freedom of grace.

The Father's justice is not a transaction; it is a transformation. It does not demand payment; it offers restoration. It is a fresh current that washes away the stale atmosphere of the courtroom. And it is always waiting, always flowing, always calling us home.

Now that you've experienced more of the courtroom with me—now that you've smelled the aged wood of the jury box and felt the heat of the room—I have to ask: Are you ready to leave yet?

The river is waiting just outside those double doors.

2

The Foundation And The Porch

HERE IS SOMETHING DEEPLY EMBEDDED IN THE human psyche that gravitates toward the cold, clinical calculus of the courtroom. It is a place of structured fear, where the air is stale with the weight of debt and the outcomes are binary: Guilty or Not Guilty. This is the world's definition of justice, and it is the spiritual architecture of the Barabbas nature we explored—transactional, adversarial, and retributive. We feel safer when there are walls, even if those walls are built to imprison us; at least in a prison, the rules are clear.

But to understand the river of reconciliation, we must immediately trade this breathless, distant judgment for a warmer, more intimate truth. We must leave the musty halls of the courthouse and find the Father. We must realize that the foundation of the throne is not a judge's bench, but a family's support. In the Hebrew mind, righteousness (*Tzedakah*) was never a grade on a test or a tally of moral successes; it was the social fiber of a right relationship. Justice (*Mishpat*) was the action taken to restore that fiber when it frayed.

If the foundation of the throne is justice and righteousness, it means the very baseline of God's authority is His commitment to keep us in The Way of His life. The Father is not waiting in the high seat of a courtroom; He is sitting on the porch. The crowd on Pilate's pavement chose the rebel because they could not conceive of a king who would not fight. They needed a messiah who made sense—one who balanced the books with a sword. But Jesus was offering something far more dangerous: a Father on a porch who had been waiting all along.

The Prodigal Son parable is Jesus's answer to the mob. Imagine he had said, "You chose the revolutionary because you thought justice meant making them pay. Let me show you what you rejected: a father who runs toward the wreckage, kills the fattened calf for the guilty, and throws a feast before a single act of penance is performed." The older brother stands outside that feast the same way the crowd stood on the pavement—furious that grace doesn't require payment, scandalized that the Father's justice looks more like a living banquet than a hollow courtroom.

The Third Son on the Porch

THIS IS THE ULTIMATE IMAGE OF GOD'S NATURE, REvealed powerfully in the Parable of The Prodigal Son. This story often teaches us to see two sons: the prodigal who strays and the older brother who stays. But to discern the Father's true heart, we must recognize the presence of a Third Son: Jesus Himself, the narrator, revealing the Father to us. Jesus, as the definitive witness, pulls us in close to recognize the eternal, unwavering nature of the Father. He is revealing the impossibility of being truly lost from the Father's perspective.

The Father did not shudder nor waver when the son turned his back. He did not change His mind about the son's worth based on the son's actions, his morality, or his choice to leave. His chair rocks upon the foundation of a justice that is as immutable as His own Being. There is a rhythm to that rocking—a steady, unhurried frequency that acts as the baseline for the universe. It is the Whistle of Reconciliation made audible. He isn't rocking in anticipation of your failure; He is rocking in the absolute certainty of your belonging. The sound doesn't demand your attention; it invites your heartbeat to sync with His. He only knows us through His Word—not a set of spoken decrees, but the Person of Christ Himself. Because Jesus is the Word made flesh, He is the living verdict of our Father. When we speak of the Word as a sword, we are describing the kinetic power of His Nature. He does not need to litigate; His Presence simply outshines the musty darkness of the audit.

I have seen this immutable love—this refusal of the Father to blink—steady a man when the world was trying to bury him. For a decade, my husband, John, had been living in the agony of a fractured perspective. He was two men in one: the partner I was desperately in love with—the one who stood with me to manage our son's insulin and handled his own legal battles with quiet strength—and a man encircled by a mirage of separation. This whispered a lie that he was a bad father because he hadn't protected our girls from a wolf he didn't know was there. He tried to drown that lie in the bottle. He drank alone, and I only ever saw the aftermath of the attempt. To watch a capable man try to drown a lie that big is a slow-motion heartbreak. I acted as the support beam for a structure that was leaning further every year.

The breaking day came just after Christmas. With family in the house, I sat just outside our bedroom, working and praying while he lay in the disarray of his lowest low. When he woke and looked at me, he saw a look that betrayed my terror; he saw I was finally losing my footing. The next morning, he drove off. We had barely shared words, but in the silence of his drive, he begged God for an end.

But God answered with a resurrection. In my husband's restoration, God didn't just issue a command from the heavens. The Living Word stepped into that truck. The hollow lie of John's failure simply could not coexist with the freshness of the Son's Presence. The sword didn't strike the man; the Word restored the man by consuming the lie that held his mind hostage. What the verdict revealed was not a sentence passed, but a person. He delivered him instantly—taking the desire for alcohol and leaving the man I had fought to stay beside.

When the Father runs toward the son, it isn't a reaction to the son's repentance, as if he finally earned a change in God's mood. It is the overflow of a love that was always there, always steady, and always in pursuit. The Father doesn't wait for a legal hearing because the verdict was never in question. He is sitting on the porch, on the threshold of His piercing love, holding fast to the truth of who the Son is in Christ. The son is not re-admitted after proving himself; he is simply recognized as the child he never stopped being. John's original design never broke; he simply finally saw the Father's face through the stagnant fog of the audit.

The Older Brother in the Courtroom

Paradoxically, the older brother has not been rocking on the porch, consumed by the simple affection of his Father. Instead, he is stewing in his own flesh, turning his inheritance—the very bounty of the Father's land—into a stale, clinical courtroom. His tragedy is that he did not hold fast to true identity. He rehearsed his sadness, churning it into anger and festering until hatred set in, causing him to disassociate from his own kin. In his mind, his brother is no longer a prodigal, but an enemy of the state. He storms the house, building a case against the brother hoping to attain what is already his.

This is the plumb line out of alignment. The older brother is using the world's transactional math to weigh his brother's failures against his own faithfulness. He thinks justice means his brother should pay, when the Father knows that justice—true *mishpat*—means the brother has been restored to the family table. Both sons received an inheritance. One spent it on reckless living, and the other turned his into a hollow courtroom. Both paths lead away from the heart of the Father.

The older brother's courtroom is a tragic distortion of the Father's justice. It is a place where love is conditional, where performance measures worth, and where the family table is replaced by a cold witness stand. He cannot see that the Father's justice is not about weighing sins but about restoring sons. The Father's heart does not divide itself because of one son's failures or the other's bitterness. His justice is not a transaction to be negotiated; it is a feast to be shared. The older brother's tragedy is not that he was left out of the celebration—it's that he stayed outside, clinging to the stagnant accounting of his own merit instead of stepping into the river.

The Cost of the Plantation

I KNOW THE COST OF THE OLDER BROTHER'S PLANTATION because I built one myself. Toward the end of a ten-year storm, desperate for an end to the addiction that had gripped my husband and the brokenness within me, I reached toward religious structures—a system of enslavement that was sure and known. Alcohol numbed my spouse, and striving drowned my pain. Before I knew it, I was neck-deep in the system, and my father—the voice I was gleaning from—was religion. I turned my back on my grace upbringing out of desperation for a controlled, predictable environment.

I was certain love possessed a backbone and that truth demanded utterance, however jagged or sharp its edge. The more rigid I became, the more I mistook my performance for maturity. I thought I was growing stronger, but inside, I was reeling —lost, hurting, afraid, and very alone. In the final years of that season, we lived unhinged. The external world mirrored our internal collapse. Our home, once a sanctuary, was on a rapid descent toward dilapidation. The roof leaked, the plumbing was persistently clogged, and the structural supports of our life seemed to rot from the inside out. Every time the rain fell, I didn't just see water on the floor; I felt it as a physical manifestation of my own leaking spirit. A condition I was too embarrassed to even acknowledge with our kids. My soul had become a reservoir for the stale water of the plantation—stagnant, backed up by the debris of religious striving. But the Father didn't come with a wrench to punish the mess; He came as the river to flush the system. He didn't wait for me to 'clear the line'; His presence simply became a pressure of love that the clogs of fear could no longer withstand.

Our home eventually went into foreclosure. We reached the point where we thought it was a lost cause; we had moved out, resigned to the heavy, cold verdict that we had failed. But amid that unraveling, God intervened in a way that bypassed the audit entirely. The county sold the house for the exact amount we owed on it–clearing the debt to the penny. In that precision, I saw a familiar signature. It was the same unwavering nature we saw in the mouth of a fish or the weight of a breaking net in the previous chapter. Just as Jesus didn't ask Peter to audit his effort before providing the temple tax or the overflowing catch, He didn't wait for my life to be tidy before He settled the account of our house. He wasn't rewarding my performance; He was revealing His character. He proved that His provision is not a transaction to be earned, but a gift to be received by those who have finally run out of their own strength. It was a miracle that left us stunned—a glimmer of fresh air that whispered the Father was still watching the road, even when we had abandoned the property.

Yet, a cleared ledger is not the same as a healed heart. Even with the debt gone, the religious atmosphere around us remained predatory. Organizations that functioned like vultures, waiting for signs of failure, surrounded us so they could parade them about like ripped flesh in the sky. When you live on a plantation, your day doesn't end when the sun goes down. It ends with the late-night audit. I remember the racing heart that tried to keep pace with my racing thoughts. Every action of my day stood before a judge. I would convict myself before the gavel could even strike. I called it discipline at the time, but I see now that it was anxiety making its abode within me. I was living by the world's weight, perpetually measuring my performance against an invisible, breathless standard I could never quite meet. The plantation promises control, but it delivers exhaustion. It offers structure, but it demands your soul.

I had become a citizen of that exhaustion. I was so used to the clinical chill of the Audit that when I finally stepped into the warmth of the Son; the transition was jarring—not just for me, but for everyone still standing in the cold. I had to learn that once you've spent years defending a plantation, the unmanaged freedom of the Porch feels like a betrayal of everything you've suffered to maintain.

The Offense of Joy

WE OFTEN THINK THE COURTROOM IS ONLY FOR THE

guilty, but the Older Brother proves you can build a trial out of your own faithfulness. His tragedy wasn't that he was a sinner; it was that his heart had become so leathered by the labor of the plantation that he could no longer stomach the scent of a feast. To a man who has spent a lifetime weighing his worth by his sweat, the unmanaged joy of a child is not an invitation—it is an offense.

I lived in the crosshairs of this collision during a season I think of as my decade of bliss. During those years, I lived in the throes of a freedom so thick it was intoxicating. I was in love with the Father, and I had simply run out of reasons not to smile. My theology wasn't a lecture; it was a perma-smile that refused to be rattled by the protocols of the religious system. I was the girl who knew the shade of the Tree of Life intimately, savoring the nectar of a God who actually liked me.

In those years, I was so intoxicated by the sheer scale of joy I experienced that it didn't even occur to me I was free. Fear causes calculating distance—worrying about your position or potential losses—but when the Son's current engulfs you, the Audit's math fails. I wasn't brave; a Reality that made the rules of the Courtroom look like a child's game simply consumed me.

But joy is an aggressive intruder on the plantation. To those whose hearts have become worn and leathered by the Audit—those who are still white-knuckling their standing—

my laughter felt like a mockery of their labor. They accused me of hiding behind a facade, because the religious mind cannot conceive of a peace that isn't earned through a grimace. At the time, I didn't appreciate how easily jaded we can become. I hadn't yet realized that for many, a cheerful heart doesn't feel like medicine—it feels like a violation.

A demand for a verdict that no amount of smiling could settle then interrupted the bliss. As the floor fell out from under us with the discovery of the systemic violation within our own family—a breach of trust so deep it dismantled the very architecture of our peace. In an instant, a jagged reality that required more than a grip on grace to survive replaced the nectar.

It was then that I discovered the true mechanical cruelty of the Older Brother. I realized that the same spirit that questioned the legitimacy of my smile was the same one that preferred I simply get over the trauma. To the auditor, both my joy and my agonizing grief were unmanaged variables that disrupted the order of the plantation. They wanted me to move on—not for the sake of my healing, but for the sake of their comfort.

In that season, I finally understood the older brother's rage. When you are drowning in a wound that runs that deep, the music and dancing of a Father who offers a feast to the undeserving can feel like a profound injustice. You want a Sword; the Father offers a seat. You want a Gavel; the Father offers a Ring.

The older brother's contract is a prison built out of the demand for a specific fairness. He stays outside the party because he cannot forgive the Father for being so easy on a world that has been so hard on him. He is the ultimate hired hand, guarding a door that the Father has already taken off its hinges, waiting for a payment that Christ has already absorbed.

This demand for a payment isn't just a personal character flaw; it is an architectural legacy. The Romans, not people on porches, established our Western concept of what is right, training us to prefer the ledger over the lap. We find it nearly impossible to rest in a Father who refuses to keep score because a system that views seeing as a liability has baptized us.

The Blindfold of Iustitia

FOR CENTURIES, MUCH OF THE WESTERN CHRISTIAN SYStem has adopted the older brother's mentality, leading many believers to live in constant fear of mis-stepping. We traded the Hebrew foundation of restorative *mishpat*—which sought to put things right—for a Roman foundation of retributive *Iustitia*—which seeks to make things pay. Lady Justice's ubiquitous statue perfectly captures this Roman legacy. We see her standing atop our courthouses, holding a balance in one hand and a Sword in the other. But the most telling feature is her blindfold. In the Roman mind, the blindfold represents impartiality. While that may be a noble goal for a human court, it is a clinical, breathless lens for the Kingdom of God.

When we project the blindfold of *Iustitia* onto the Father, we create a God who refuses to see His children. We imagine a Judge who is intentionally ignoring our original design to focus solely on the performance of our lives. We think He is weighing our debt in the dark, ready to swing the Sword the moment the balance shifts. But the Father on the Porch has no blindfold. His justice doesn't come from closing His eyes to the offender; it comes from fixing His gaze upon the child. Where *Iustitia* is blind to the person in order to be fair, the Father is hyper-aware of the person in order to be restorative. He doesn't want to balance a ledger; He wants to lock eyes with you. He isn't looking at the record or files; He is looking at the child He never took His eyes off.

The Architecture of Satisfaction

WHEN I FIRST ENCOUNTERED THE LOGIC OF OFFENDED honor, I didn't realize I was being handed a feudal contract instead of a Father's invitation. This grimacing news, hinging on luck, felt more like a game of roulette where my heart was the currency, and the rigged requirements were in play. Total offense.

This Roman shift was first formalized in the eleventh century by a theologian named Anselm of Canterbury. Living in a world of feudal lords and rigid social hierarchies, Anselm argued that human sin had offended God's honor, and like a debt to a king, it required a satisfaction that only a divine death could provide.

This birthed the doctrine known as Penal Substitutionary Atonement (PSA). It presented the image of an angry God who just needed to hit something—a Divine Judge whose holy rage was so combustible that it had to be diverted onto a substitute to keep the universe from imploding.

Centuries later, the Reformers, particularly John Calvin, expanded and cemented this legal framework. Although I can survey my past and detect where this mindset revealed itself, I didn't formally encounter the system until recently. The introduction was cold and arrogant—a clinical attempt to get me saved although I had been in ministry for over twenty years. In that environment, my experience of walking with the Father was irrelevant; my inability to recite the TULIP doctrine was presented as the only evidence of my doom.

Calvin, who was himself trained as a lawyer, took Anselm's offended honor and turned it into divine jurisprudence. Calvin's legal framework is brilliant if you're a lawyer, but it's suffocating if you're a daughter. It's the reason my shoulders used to hunch in corporate times of prayer—I was bracing for a deposition, not a conversation. In Calvin's view, God was the Supreme Legislator, and the Cross was the Supreme Courtroom. He argued Christ had to absorb God's holy anger against sin, diverting the outpouring from us onto himself. This suggests that blood must spill to appease God.

This is where the 'Legalized Gospel' became the very air we breathe in the West, reducing our oxygen, leaving us aching for fresh wind beyond the smog of religion. It is why so many of us spend our lives white-knuckling a grip on grace. A lawyer has trained us to approach a Father as if He were a Judge. This is precisely why you nervously visit the Porch with your legal briefs tucked under your arm, ready to litigate your right to be there.

While the traditional frameworks of substitution or ransom have been used for centuries to explain this moment, they often fail to capture the full, staggering weight of the wreckage. The Cross was not a legal settlement to appease a distant God; it was the Father's ultimate 'I am here' in the middle of our self-made hell. He didn't send Jesus to pay a debt He was holding against us; He came in Christ to absorb the violence we were holding against ourselves. It wasn't about a Judge getting His due; it was about a Father getting His children back.. We were at our absolute worst—so colonized by the knowledge of good and evil that when Love made flesh walked into the room without a ledger, we didn't know how to receive Him. In our delusion, a love like Christ's made little sense; it was a threat to the only system of control we knew.

The Cross exposed the religious worst in the Pharisee who needed a rule to feel safe. It exposed the political worst in the leader who needed power to feel secure. And it exposed the internal worst in all of us—the part of the human soul that would rather kill Love than accept a seat it didn't earn.

But the Father answered our violence with a reality that was, as Paul writes in Romans 5, *out of all proportion to our trespass.* The audit is a one-to-one accounting; it demands an eye for an eye. But the Gift is not like the debt. If our worst was capable of killing Love, the Father's response was a landslide of grace that didn't just cover an offense—it buried the entire geography of our rebellion and raised us up in life full tilt.

God saw the wreckage of our ability to even want Him. He knew that the only way to reach us was to let our violence spend itself on His own heart. He entered our darkest hour, not to satisfy an offended ego, but to witness our wreckage and blow the doors off the prison from the inside. So that we could cease shadowboxing a Judge and start receiving a nonsensical, unearned love that is, frankly, completely intimidating to a mind that still wants to pay its own way, he died. The Gift is so massive that it doesn't just pay the debt—it bankrupts the entire system of debt itself.

When you finally step onto the Porch, the fire of God doesn't consume you; it consumes the paperwork. It incinerates every stale, clinical legal brief you brought to prove your worthiness, leaving only the unadorned, indivisible child.

The Bēma: The Victor's Platform

IF THE CROSS WAS THE FINAL LANDSLIDE THAT BURIED the geography of our debt, then we must re-evaluate every scene we've cast in the shadows of a future judgment. Many of us live with a low-grade fever of anxiety regarding the final audit, as if the Father's yes at the Cross were merely a temporary stay of execution. We imagine standing before a magistrate who is finally ready to read the fine print of our failures. But once the Son incinerates the paperwork, the seat of authority entirely changes its nature.

The Apostle Paul spoke of the Bēma (2 Corinthians 5:10). The Bēma is a Platform of Truth, not a Court of fear. In the Greco-Roman world, the *bēma* was an award platform or a review stand—a place of honor and public declaration of results. To grasp the relief of this truth, trade the image of a magistrate's bench for that of an Olympic award ceremony. It is the place where the fire of His presence doesn't look for what is wrong, but burns away everything that isn't you, leaving only the gold of your original design. Guilt or innocence aren't being decided; that verdict was already delivered at the Cross.

Instead, the Bēma is the Victor's Platform. You don't stand at the Bēma to be audited for your flaws; you stand there to be celebrated for your Union. The 'Fire' of that moment isn't a punitive heat; it's the warmth of the Porch light, burning away every lingering shadow of the 'Adam' until all that remains is the gold of who the Father always knew you were. It's not a day of reckoning; it's a day of recognition. The original verb for receive back is *komisētai*. While many translations say to receive what is due, the Greek means to carry off a reward. The goal is not condemnation for failures, but the Father acknowledging and rewarding faithful actions while the failures are cleansed in the light of His conquering sacrifice. The Bēma is the ultimate declaration of the Father's heart: a place of celebration, not fear. When the Victor's Platform becomes the Father's Porch, it reminds us we were never running to earn His approval. We were running to Him all along.

The Bureaucracy of the Grave

A NEW LEGALISM HAS CREPT INTO THE PRAYER LIVES OF the weary. Many have been told they must traverse courts of

Heaven to identify generational loopholes and litigate their way into freedom that was supposedly already bought. This is a technical ritual masquerading as high-level intercession. It suggests that the Cross was a legal theory that requires our constant, manual enforcement to be effective. It turns the believer into a spiritual paralegal, endlessly filing paperwork to get a Judge to notice a squatter on their land.

But if distance is a lie, then we do not need to travel to a courtroom to find the Judge. If the enemy is a paraded fool, he was already publicly shamed 2,000 years ago. True spiritual authority isn't about the complexity of your legal argument; it's about the simplicity of your original design. You don't bring an enemy to justice; you bring the Just One into the room. When you lock eyes with Jesus, the paraded fools become a footnote. We aren't suing for peace; we are standing in a verdict that has no appeals process.

Justice That Seeks Wholeness: Romans 5:18

WORLDLY JUSTICE SEEKS TO MAKE THINGS PAY; DIVINE justice seeks to make things whole. This is the heartbeat of Romans 5:18. In Greek, the word for justification used here—*dikaiōsis*—refers to the act of pronouncing someone righteous, a judicial verdict of acquittal. But Paul couples it with life. This is the Father standing on the porch and legally decreeing that the fracture of the Fall is over. He isn't just clearing your criminal record; He is restoring your perspective. He is saying that Christ's one righteous act has set the plumb line straight in your sight again.

Adam's trespass did not—and could not—bring a death of our being; we were always the spoken Word of God made flesh, and that origin was perpetually safe in God's hands. What Adam brought was a catastrophic mental breakdown. We were only ever enemies in our own minds; the enmity was never on God's end (Colossians 1:21). Convinced we were separate from our Source, we suffered a dislocation of the soul, a spiritual amnesia. We spent centuries building a hollow courtroom to hide from a Father who was only ever looking for a dinner date. Christ's justification of life brings a reclamation of our original state. It isn't a change in your essence, but a restoration of your awareness.

The Original Trick: Becoming What You Are

THE SERPENT'S VICTORY WAS GETTING ADAM AND EVE TO internalize the lie of attainment, the false gospel that their likeness was something to be earned, striven for, or seized through an external act, rather than something that was their inherent birthright. He convinced them they were lacking, and the moment they believed in their own lack, the courtroom was born.

They moved from the rest of the Porch to the labor of the plantation, trying to become what they already were.

The serpent's promise—*You will be like God, knowing good and evil*, was the original Barabbas choice. He was offering Adam and Eve the power to determine justice for themselves. To know good and evil is to have the authority to weigh, measure, and demand payment. It's the promise of the world's transactional math. Eve chose what the crowd would choose—the stale fruit of autonomy, the exhausting burden of self-determination. She chose the rebel's logic: 'I will balance this myself.' And we've been standing on that platform ever since, rejecting the King who offers rest for the revolutionary who offers control.

The Altar Call Agony: Audition At The Altar

For many of us, the cycle of striving began at the altar. I recently found myself overcome with emotion as I reflected on what getting saved was actually like for me as a teenager. It wasn't a moment of peace; it was a season of prolonged spiritual uncertainty. I remember the smell of the old church —a mix of dust and wax—and the way the soft music would vibrate through the soles of my shoes during the invitation. The weight of the atmosphere was heavy and thick with the implication that my destiny hung on the razor's edge of my own sincerity.

I never knew whether I had done it right. This led to a quiet, desperate routine: I would respond to every altar call for salvation, week after week. Every time I walked down that aisle, I was trying to bribe a Judge I didn't realize had already closed the case. I viewed the Father as a magistrate of 'Maybe,' but He is actually the Judge of 'It is Finished.' I was attempting to get a 'Yes' that He had spoken over me before the stars were born. The Father wasn't looking at my 'sincerity' to see if it met a shifting threshold; He was looking at the Lamb and seeing the Verdict of my inclusion. The altar wasn't a place to change the Judge's mind; it was a place where the Judge was finally changing mine. But I wasn't seeking intimacy with a Father, I was trying to avoid the fear of eternal separation. That is not a description of love. That is a description of torment. At every altar call, I was unknowingly choosing the certainty of striving over the freedom of trust.

I sat in those pews, trembling under the weight of my own no—my fear, my doubt, and my frantic attempts to secure a salvation I thought was fragile. I believed my yes was the key to the door. But I didn't realize that while I was stuttering through a prayer, the Father's Yes was already roaring over me. He didn't wait for my sincerity to be perfect; He had already decided I was His. Reality had already caught me up in the Father's heart, even though my teenage audition responded to a hallucination of distance.

The Counsel of Eternity

To break the cycle of striving, we must anchor ourselves in the Counsel of Eternity. Revelation 13:8 states that the Lamb was slain before the foundation of the world. This verse utterly dismantles the idea of a reactive God. Time does not bind the Almighty. For us, the cross is an event that happened two thousand years ago; for God, the cross is an eternal reality.

The moment God purposed to create you—knowing every doubt you would wrestle with—He simultaneously purposed the solution. This truth reframes the entire narrative of justice. The worldly courtroom acts after the crime, demanding payment. Before the crime occurs, the Father performs acts of reconciliation, ensuring His children return before they even stray. The cross was not a repair job; it was the blueprint. The Lamb kept you safe before the Garden ever lost you.

The Difference Between a Pardon and a New Being

The fundamental lie that keeps us striving is the belief that salvation is merely a legal pardon—amnesty. While this legal reality is part of the story, if it stands alone, it reinforces fear. If salvation is only a pardon, you remain fundamentally a pardoned criminal—perpetually afraid of committing the next offense. You are a person with a clean record but a broken nature, living in a state of permanent spiritual probation.

But the plan of the Lamb was profoundly deeper than a legal pardon. It was a change of being—a complete restoration of who you were. The cross was therefore the ultimate act of reclaiming our design: the moment where the divine nature of Christ fully merged with human nature, rendering it incorruptible. It shattered the lie of attainment, securing our likeness to God not as something we must strive for, but as something we already are in Christ.

The Father on the Porch was never waiting for you to say the prayer right at an altar call. He was already holding the robe and the ring, because the Lamb had already settled the issue of your nature. You are not just a forgiven sinner trying to keep your record clean; you are a new creation with the very life of God flowing through your veins. The audition is over. You don't have to work to be like God anymore; you simply rest in the truth that He has already made you like Himself.

3

The End Of Bureaucracy

The Sanctuary of the Cage

I F GOD MADE US LIKE HIM, WHY DO WE STILL FEEL like we are navigating a maze of red tape? We talk about being born again, but then spend our days filling out spiritual forms in triplicate, waiting for a stamp of approval from a God who has already moved into our skin (Colossians 1:27). The moment we forget our rebirth, we build scaffolds to reach a Father who is already holding us. We trade the organic rhythm of the house for a spiritual bureaucracy—a system of rules, intermediaries, and protocols that promises safety but delivers distance.

As soon as we accept that the Lamb was slain before the foundation of the world (Revelation 13:8), we can dismantle every religious scaffold we have built to explain away the perceived harshness of God. If Jesus is the exact representation of the Father's being—the only one who has truly seen Him (Hebrews 1:3)—then we have to reconcile the God on the Porch with the God of lightning and thunder. The truth is, the Father never changed His mood; we changed our jurisdiction.

I once saw the condition of the religious mind as a series of prison cells—dirty, dark, and lifeless. People crammed in, body on body; the room reeked of apathy. But as I looked closer, the most staggering part wasn't the filth; it was the fact that the prison doors were standing wide open. These men and women were captive only in their minds. They had been sold a lie that the cell was life and the hallway was a threat. The bureaucracy had become a sanctuary—a predictable cage.

Freedom is the scariest thing you will ever pursue. It removes the safety of the walls we used to define ourselves. When humanity stepped away from the Porch in the garden, we didn't step into a vacuum; we stepped into a Bureaucracy. We were like those prisoners—too embarrassed to look in God's direction and too terrified of a love so vast it doesn't need to manage us. Stepping into the Father's unhurried rhythm felt like a threat, given how accustomed we were to the 'safety' of the bars. We didn't realize the door wasn't just an exit from a cell; it was the entrance to a Feast. We preferred the predictable bondage of Egypt over the scary freedom of the Father's bread (Exodus 16:3).

The seduction of Egypt is not only about leeks and onions; it's about the comfort of the predictable (Numbers

11:5). In bondage, the terms are simple. You know the cost of your survival, even if it's measured in straw and mud. We have a strange habit of preferring a taskmaster we can manage over a Father who wants to care for us. In the audit, we are the ones who hold the ledger. Even if the balance is always in the red, we feel a sense of agency in our own suffering.

Walking through that open prison door means stepping into a world where our performance is no longer the currency. That is the true terror of freedom. The system, which dislikes us, prefers to sustain us rather than be liberated by a Father who adores us, as the system's regulations are simpler to classify than a Love that refuses to keep score (1 Corinthians 13:5). The organic rhythm of a Father's house was traded for the clinical management of a system. We needed the Law not because God wanted a barrier, but because we wanted a buffer. We were so convinced of our own separation that we reached for rules, regulations, and intermediaries to manage the chaos of our fractured hearts.

The thunder on Sinai was not the Father's heart; it was the sound of a world groaning under the weight of the bureaucracy it had chosen.

The Security Guard Era

I'M NOT PROPOSING A NEW DOCTRINE HERE; I'M USING AN

image to describe how a mediated, fear-based relationship with God feels from the inside.

The first clue to the distance of the Law lies in its delivery. We often imagine God leaning over the balcony of heaven, pressing tablets into Moses' hands in a warm, face-to-face exchange. Paul and the writer of Hebrews both point this out not as a strange trivia point, but to show that the Law came as a mediated covenant—through angels and Moses—rather than the direct, face-to-face knowing we see in Jesus (Galatians 3:19, Hebrews 2:2). The Law was the Father's way of keeping a roof over our heads while we were still too afraid to come inside the House. He didn't delegate our care to 'security guards,' because He was distant; He commissioned their protection because we were terrified. The Law wasn't a barrier He built to keep us out; it was a buffer He allowed to keep us safe until we could handle the 'high-voltage' reality of His unedited embrace. The angels were not a replacement for His presence, but a scaffolding for our fragility.

This is not an insignificant detail; it signals a jurisdiction. The Law came to us through what I call the Security Guard Era. We had asked for a manager, and heaven honored our request. The people who trembled at Sinai begged Moses, *You speak to us... but do not let God speak to us, lest we die* (Exodus 20:19). We see the same pattern when Israel demanded a king.

God warned a king would build a tax-heavy bureaucracy, take their sons and fields, and draft their lives into his project (1 Samuel 8:10-18). *But the people insisted: No! But there shall be a king over us, that we also may be like all the nations.* We wanted the audit of a kingdom we could see more than the Porch of a Father we had to trust.

By choosing the transactional path of autonomy, mankind stepped out from simple trust and into a layered world of powers and authorities—what Scripture hints at as thrones, dominions, and rulers (Colossians 1:16)—real spiritual influences that were never meant to replace the Father, only to serve within His love. When we walked away from trust, the birthright fell into the dust. I sometimes imagine that the loyal angelic orders—the ones who remained true to the Father—stepped in not as new gods, but as emergency guardians of a territory we had abandoned.

Imagine an elite security firm hired to manage a playground because the parents walked away. They can enforce rules, stop fights, and keep everyone inside the fence. But they cannot love the children. They manage behavior through the threat of the ledger, but they can never recognize the being of the child. That's the atmosphere of the Law: a necessary, ironclad structure to keep the playground from collapsing before the Seed of Judah (Genesis 49:10) could arrive and walk us home.

We often mistake the intensity of that security firm for ultimate spiritual authority. I remember a weekend spent among those who deemed themselves experts in high-level spiritual warfare. The room pulsed with restless energy—a constant, competitive jostling for the top dog of discernment. As the experts performed their maneuvers, a chaotic crazy manifested in the atmosphere. I felt profoundly out of place, as if I were a guest at a deposition I hadn't prepared for. In the middle of that swirl, the Father whispered a phrase that redefined the arena: 'Those who play in the second heavens—the jurisdiction where we attempt to audit darkness rather than rest in the Light—pay in the second heavens.'

It was a jurisdictional warning. When I say second heaven here, I'm not drawing a cosmic map; I'm talking about an inner world—a mindset of mediation and spiritual performance where everything feels measured, categorized, and contested. When we try to gain spiritual ground by becoming better managers of darkness—more precise auditors of demonic activity—we are checking ourselves back into the courthouse. We are playing a game where the currency is still striving. The Father was holding my feet to a different arena: the simple ground of shared stories, smiles, and tears. He

wasn't asking me to become an expert on shadows; He was inviting me to remain a daughter in the Light.

There is a profound difference between being policed and
being parented. The loyal orders weren't being cruel; they were
being legal. They were containment specialists, ensuring that
the musty basement of the audit didn't crumble into total
chaos before the Son arrived. Their Biology adjusted to transactional justice—the kind that identifies wrongdoing, quanti-
fies the offense, and guarantees punishment. They were
administrators of the math we had demanded.

A security guard's watch makes a child constantly aware of
her behavior. She checks her proximity to the rules, calculating
every move. When a parent holds that same child, she is aware
only of her being. The guard sees a subject to be managed; the
Father sees a son or daughter to be enjoyed. The atmosphere of
the Law carried the metallic chill of the guard's gaze. It could
keep the playground safe, but it could never make the children
feel at home. It was a jurisdiction of compliance, protecting
the bloodline while the Father waited for the day He could
step back onto the field Himself.

The Perspective of the Fire

IF JESUS IS THE EXACT REPRESENTATION OF THE FATHER'S
being (Hebrews 1:3), and God is the same yesterday, today,

and forever (Hebrews 13:8), then we have to reconsider Sinai. What if the lightning and thunder weren't a change in God's mood, but a collision between His unchanging love and our distorted perspective?

Before Jesus, humanity viewed the Father through the lens of debt. Humanity viewed the Father through the lens of debt before Jesus. We held the conviction that we were His enemies (Colossians 1:21). When you believe you are an enemy, the embrace of a Father feels like the grip of a Judge.

Imagine a child who has lived in the dark for so long that her eyes have adjusted to the absence of light. When a parent finally opens the curtains, the child doesn't experience morning. She experiences pain. She screams and covers her eyes, calling the sun an intruder. The sun hasn't changed its nature; it is simply being itself. The 'pain' is not the sun's cruelty, but the shadow's protest. But to a body addicted to shadows, the light feels like a threat. The child hears the Father's whistle from the porch and mistakes it for a warning siren because the cage's frequency tunes her ears. She hasn't yet learned that the sound of the whistle is the sound of the door standing open.

What if Sinai was the Father passing by, and the terror was simply how perfect Love feels to a mind convinced of its own separation? For the son who knows he is loved, that fire represents bliss. To the mind trapped in the audit, that same fire feels like a threat (Hebrews 12:28-29).

But even in the middle of the bureaucracy, the Father was accessible. Moses spoke with God *face to face, as a man speaks to his friend* (Exodus 33:11). David danced with an unedited delight that paid no attention to protocol (2 Samuel 6:14). They prove that the bureaucracy was a buffer for the fearful, not a barrier for the Father. God was never the one locking the cells; we were the ones refusing to believe the door was already standing open.

The Memo from the Front Lines

I FELT THE WEIGHT OF THIS SPIRITUAL BUREAUCRACY most clearly during a season I often think of as my decade of bliss. I was in my thirties, and for the first time, the low-grade fever of my youth—that constant worry about my standing— finally broke. I was living in the rhythm of a God who actually liked me.

During those years, the very air of my life changed. My prayer life shifted from a series of desperate petitions and exhausting audits to a quiet, ongoing conversation that didn't require me to clear my throat or fix my face. I laughed more. I lingered over the mundane. I realized the Father wasn't just observing my life from a distance; He was taking part in it with me. I wasn't trying to gain entry anymore; I was living like someone who already had the keys and could use them (Matthew 16:19).

In the middle of that freedom, I received a note from someone who felt compelled to address my state. The message read: "You are out of control! Thus saith the Lord."

The words landed like a boundary line drawn around my heart. In the world of bureaucracy, the worst thing a child can be is unmanaged. The message wasn't born of malice; it was born of a mindset that values order and predictability above all else. He saw a daughter caught in a rhythm he didn't recognize, and because the world of the audit requires everyone to walk in straight lines, he mistook my delight for a lack of discipline.

This is the quiet tragedy of the religious mind: we try to fix the very joy the Father is currently enjoying. We feel a pull to draw the out of control child back toward the plantation, where behavior is easier to measure. But that is the clatter of the spiritual bureaucracy trying to maintain its borders. It cannot comprehend the freedom of the Porch.

I weighed that note. I wondered if my freedom had become a stumbling block, if my laughter was irresponsible. The Father offered a different perspective through a friend who asked me, "Angie, when a father is tossing his kid high into the air, who is in control?"

In a single sentence, the scene shifted. My joy wasn't uncontrolled; it was being held. I was out of control only in the sense that I had surrendered to One who is always in control. The middle-managers of the spirit want us to march so they can measure our progress. The Father simply wants us to take part in the dance.

The Peacocking Middle-Man

WE SEE THE LINGERING EFFECTS OF THIS SPIRITUAL BUReaucracy in the posturing that dominates religious culture today. Systems love a middle-man because middle-men love titles. They need visible badges—'strong leader,' 'pillar of the community,' 'anointed vessel'—to justify their place at the table (Matthew 23:5-7).

When we label someone this way, we're often issuing a performance grade. Strong becomes shorthand for 'useful to the system.' Anointed becomes a way to say, 'You're producing results we can count on.' This need to label is a cover for insecurity—a way to prove we're 'in' so we don't have to face the terrifying possibility of being unmanaged.

But the Father on the Porch doesn't want a strong leader. He wants His child. A son does not need an adjective to belong. He does not need a title to sit at the table. He just needs to be a son (Romans 8:15).

There are places in the Old Testament that still make my mind itch and my stomach tighten. I don't have neat answers for all of them, but I have learned where to anchor my trust.

The Law Outside the Ark

IF YOU FEEL LIKE YOU'RE BEING YANKED BETWEEN TWO different versions of God—the one who runs to prodigals and the one who strikes Uzzah for touching the Ark—you're not imagining the tension. It's the whiplash of trying to breathe in two atmospheres at once: the Porch of Jesus and the bureaucracy of the Law.

Hidden in Israel's story is a quiet clue that has given my heart more rest than any clever explanation. When Moses finished writing the Law, God gave a very specific instruction: *Take this Book of the Law and put it by the side of the Ark of the Covenant of the Lord your God, that it may be there for a witness against you* (Deuteronomy 31:26). The core testimony of the covenant—the tablets—rested inside the Ark, under the mercy seat. The 603 additional commands the layers of regulation Israel carried were stored beside it as a witness against them. They were not the heartbeat in the center; they were the record of a people who kept demanding more structure than trust.

Jeremiah pulls that curtain back even farther. Speaking on God's behalf, he says, *For I did not speak to your fathers or command them concerning burnt offerings and sacrifices on the day that I brought them out of the land of Egypt. But this is what I commanded them, saying, 'Obey My voice, and I will be your God, and you shall be My people* (Jeremiah 7:22-23). In other words, God's first word to His people was not, 'Here is how to keep Me from killing you with sacrifices.' His first word was, 'Walk with Me, and let Me be your God.' We have to ask: Where did the blood and the bureaucracy come from if God didn't ask for it? Israel had spent 400 years in the shadow of Egypt—a world where gods were transactional and love had a price tag. When they stood before the God at Sinai, they couldn't handle a Father who just wanted a walk on the Porch; they defaulted to the only language they knew: the language of the 'Taskmaster.'

God is stunningly blunt through Jeremiah: He didn't ask for a slaughterhouse; He asked for a conversation. The 603 regulations weren't a divine 'wish list'; they were a set of 'guardrails' for a people who were so addicted to the Egyptian math of sacrifice that they couldn't conceive of a God who just wanted their company. The blood on the floor wasn't for His satisfaction; it was a concession to their own conviction that love must be bought. The Law, a witness to our fear, not a map of His heart, resided outside the Ark.

That doesn't make stories like Uzzah's less painful. Uzzah was the man who reached out to steady the Ark when the oxen stumbled and fell dead on the spot (2 Samuel 6:6-7). I don't pretend to have a tidy answer for that moment, and I no longer try to explain it away. Uzzah's death wasn't an act of divine 'anger'; it was the tragic friction of a system that Israel had asked for. When you choose to live in a 'Bureaucracy of Distance,' the very Presence that is your warmth becomes a 'Voltage' your fragile, fear-based scaffolding cannot carry. God didn't 'strike' Uzzah to make a point; Uzzah stepped into the raw, unedited Current of a Life he was trying to manage with a 'Security Guard' mindset. The Ark was never meant to be handled casually. This wasn't because God is fragile, but because Israel had agreed to live under a system where touching the symbol of His presence meant they stepped into a realm their conscience couldn't carry.

So when my heart feels that yo-yo between Jesus' unarmed embrace and the Old Testament's severe moments, I no longer conclude the Father has two faces. I conclude that I'm watching the same Love express itself inside a legal scaffolding it never wanted in the first place. Jesus is not the soft side of

God; He is the only face the Father has ever had. And if anything in the story feels unlike Him, I assume I'm seeing Love refracted through a system it came to fulfill and retire (Romans 10:4), not the revelation of a different God.

The Revoked Memo

WE HAVE TO BE HONEST: THERE ARE PARTS OF THE OLD Testament that feel contradictory. We see the God who walks in the cool of the day with Adam, and we see scenes that read like cold judicial executions. It can make your mind itch. We try to reconcile the Father we see in Jesus with the heavy-handedness of the Law, and we find ourselves back in the internal courtroom, trying to make the math work.

I could spend years dissecting every hard verse or building an intellectual case to show why the scary parts aren't actually scary. I could try to justify every apparent incongruence. But that would just make me another middle-man standing between you and the Origin. If you're wrestling with the parts of the story that don't seem to make sense, don't look to a book—not even this one—to solve it.

Just go ask Him.

He isn't hiding behind a technicality, and your confusion does not offend Him. If the distance is a lie, then you don't need me to translate His heart for you. Move past the arguments and the apologetics and ask the Father yourself. He's right there, leaning against the railing of the Porch, waiting for you to bring the mess to Him. He is unhurried, unbothered by your itching mind, and ready to show you the exact representation of His being in the face of His Son.

The Cross was the definitive act that declared: The transaction is over (John 19:30). The Father is done with the middle-men. When the veil was torn (Matthew 27:51), it wasn't just to let God out; it was to fire the security firm and dismantle the toll booths. The iron gate has been pulled off its hinges. The memo has been revoked.

You are no longer bound by a system of control. You are free to be 'out of control' in the hands of the Father, where joy, trust, and love are the only measures that matter. The bureaucracy has been bypassed. The Porch is the only jurisdiction left.

Are you ready to leave the office? The same God who once felt dangerous behind the files now stands on the Porch with His arms open—and He looks exactly like Jesus. The door is already open, and the porch light is on.

4

The Breaking Point

THERE COMES A MOMENT WHEN THE WEIGHT OF striving becomes unbearable. For some, it's a slow erosion—a quiet, persistent ache that grows louder with every failed attempt to measure up. For others, it's a sudden collapse, when the machinery of effort finally buckles under its own weight.

For me, it was both. I had spent years learning the mathematics of the Kingdom. I had reached a point where I believed that to be a loyal follower of Christ, I had to become an expert in two things: obedience and sacrifice. My focus was no longer on the person of Jesus alone, but on the precision of my own surrender. I was constantly looking for ways to go lower, convinced that the door is in the floor. If I could just diminish myself enough, I thought, I would finally find the entry point to the rest I craved.

But there is a subtle danger in self-imposed lowliness. I was attempting to gain by living without. I mistook my lack for spiritual depth, unaware that I was presenting my scars to the Father as if they were credentials for entry. I was treating my pain like a ticket I had to punch. But the Father doesn't read legal briefs of bruising; He only reads the heartbeat of His child. He wasn't looking for proof of my 'depth'; He was looking for the eyes of His daughter. He didn't want my sacrifice; He wanted my presence. We have an uncanny way of turning our tribulations into doctrine and our pain into a platform, as if the Father required a certain amount of scarring before He would allow us onto the Porch.

We often romanticize our suffering because it feels like a down payment on God's attention. In the Audit's world, pain is a currency we understand. We think if we can just prove we are sufficiently miserable or adequately broken, we might finally earn a seat at the table. It is the ultimate religious irony: we use the very things that hurt us to build a pedestal for our own humility. We aren't actually looking at the Father; we are looking at our own scars to see if they are deep enough to pass the inspection. This self-inflicted digging is exhausting because the hole never feels deep enough. I was so busy digging through the floor that I couldn't see the door was already standing wide open.

The harder I worked at my own sacrifice, the more elusive that rest became. The requirements demanded more than I had to give, and I felt the widening gap between the woman I was and the sacrifice I thought I needed to be. And then, in a season defined by the quiet accumulation of that weight, the shovel hit rock bottom.

The Revelation of the Flow

It wasn't a dramatic moment. There was no thunderclap, no voice from heaven. It was quieter than that—a "still, small voice" that whispered, "You don't have to do this anymore." At first, I didn't believe it. I had lived within the walls of effort so long I couldn't imagine life without the shovel. But the voice persisted, gentle and unrelenting: 'The current is already moving. You don't have to earn what has already been given.'

That was the moment the walls fell. I saw that the God I was attempting to please wasn't standing behind a marble bench, waiting to weigh my deeds or check the depth of my sacrifice. He was on the Porch, watching the horizon, waiting for me to stop digging.

Justice wasn't a flood of judgment coming to sweep me away; it was a deep, restorative current flowing from His heart to mine. It wasn't a destination I had to reach or a state I had to achieve—it was a presence that had been carrying me even when I was too busy white-knuckling my own survival to notice. I was finally moving from the stress of survival to the safety of union. I realized I wasn't the one providing the energy for my relationship with the Father; I was simply the one being invited to stop swimming upstream and let the water carry me.

My spiritual life had felt like a series of heavy, rusted gears that required constant oiling. My prayer life was the pump, my service was the piston, and my frantic obedience was the fuel. If one part stopped moving, I feared the entire system would seize up, leaving me stranded in the dark. But a current doesn't require a hand-crank. A river doesn't ask for your permission to flow; it moves because of its own weight and direction.

We've spent decades in the church obsessing over old to new wineskins as if the primary goal was a better external container—a better system, a better service, or a better brand of sacrifice. We were only comfortable looking at the exteriors because the exterior is something we can manage. But God was never primarily concerned with the stitching of the skin; He was always talking about the heart. He isn't looking for a more efficient way to package your effort; He is looking for a heart that has finally run out of effort so it can finally house His life.

The Living Room Liturgy

I REMEMBER SITTING IN THE QUIET OF MY LIVING ROOM, the exhaustion of my latest striving cycle finally catching up to me. I had been trying to pray, but the words felt hollow, like they were bouncing off the ceiling. I felt drained in my body, emotions, and spirit.

For me, this wasn't a one time event that happened years ago; it is a reality I have flexed in and out of for most of my adult life. Even after years of pastoring and writing, I still instinctively reach for the shovel. I still catch myself trying to 'go lower' or 'sacrifice more' to manage the Father's gaze.

And then, in the stillness of that room, I felt the shift. It wasn't loud. My attention was not required. It was just there, steady and unchanging, like a heartbeat I had finally stopped talking long enough to hear. In that moment, I realized that grace wasn't a prize to be gripped; grace was the pair of arms already holding me. I didn't have to climb a ladder or dig through the floor to reach the Father—I was already in Him, and He was in me.

The turning point wasn't a rescue of my old self; it was the kindness of the grave. I have preached for years that we must stop grave-robbing our own bodies—stop trying to crawl out of the very death that sets us free. In that living room, I finally met a love kind enough to stand over my grave and keep me from crawling back out into the audit. I had to let the expert drown so that the Son could finally live.

I realized that the wineskin the church obsesses over is actually an inside job. It wasn't enough for God to get me out of the courthouse; He had to get the courthouse out of me. As long as the courtroom remains in my heart, I will always find a way to turn the Porch into a plantation. I will try to manage the wine. But the restoration wasn't an improvement of my old life; it was the arrival of a New Life that didn't need my help to exist. The Prodigal had to die to his autonomy to return home, and he died even deeper when he met the Father's embrace and realized that his servant speech—his last attempt to manage the outcome—was irrelevant.

The Invitation to See

THIS IS THE PIVOT. IT'S NOT A CALL TO TRY HARDER, DO better, or sacrifice more—it is a sovereign invitation to awaken from the delusion. For too long, we have lived in a hallucination of distance. We have behaved like orphans while sitting at the King's table, and we have lived like defendants while the Judge was busy preparing a feast in our honor.

An orphan spends their life scanning the room for exits and checking the locks, convinced that their seat at the table is conditional on their behavior. When we live in the hallucination of distance, we treat the Father like a "landlord" rather than a "Home." We are constantly waiting for the eviction notice of our own perceived failures to be taped to the door. We think the turning point is a journey we have to take to get to

God, but it's actually the moment we realize the journey was a ghost story we told ourselves in the dark.

In reality, you are already home. The audit is over. Another has met the requirements. You don't have to audition for a love that was secured before you were born. The delusion whispered that you were separate, but Reality declares you are Indivisibly One.

As you step into the next part of this journey, I invite you to drop the bags. Drop the shovel, the shame, and the legal briefs. Awaken to the current that has been carrying you even when you were dreaming of drowning.

The Father is on the Porch, and He's been humming your name since the beginning.

PART II
THE FLOOD AND THE KISS

When justice stops being a sentence and starts being a song.

The world demands a flood of retribution to feel balanced, but the Father offers a river of restoration to make us whole. Let's stop trying to shout over the noise and instead learn the rhythm of the current that carries us.

5

A River That Doesn't Condemn

The Crisis of Recognition

WHEN YOU FINALLY HEAR THAT HUM FOR yourself, your eyes change. You realize that if the Father isn't auditing you; He isn't auditing the person standing next to you, either. But here is where the indivisibly one reality gets tested: we must move from the individual peace of the Porch to the corporate flow of the river.

If the Fall in the Garden was a crisis of individual identity—a forgetting of our origin in the Father—then what we often call the corporate fall is the crisis of how we belong to one another. We never actually lost our seat on the Porch; the Father never gave our place away. But in our spiritual amnesia, we abandoned the rest that belonged to us and began to wander.

In forgetting our connection to the Father, we also lost our sense of safety with one another. We traded the indivisibly one reality of the Family for the calculated inclusion of the tribe. Instead of seeing our brother or sister through the Father's eyes, we measured their worth through the lens of a relentless, transactional system. We started asking, "Are they safe enough to let in?" or "Have they earned their place at this table?"

This shift from Family to Tribe changed the way we relate to one another. Unconditional belonging forms the basis of the Family, whereas the Tribe functions on conditional acceptance. It weighs, measures, and decides who is in and who is out based on compliance. To understand how this manifests in the real world—and how we return to the unhurried rest of the Porch—we must look at the difference between a Flood and a river.

The Anatomy of the Flood

THE MOB THAT ROARED FOR THE RELEASE OF THE REBEL IN Jerusalem was a flood—a massive, unbanked surge of humanity driven by pressure rather than purpose. When Pilate asked them to choose, they didn't deliberate; they surged. This happens when religious tribalism takes over: it becomes a flash flood of zeal that will destroy the person just to satisfy the system.

There is a holy ache within this movement—a legitimate desire to see the world's heavy accounts balanced for the oppressed. This is the Father's own heartbeat for the broken. But the peril lies in the water's source. When social justice operates as a flood, it becomes a manic, shared adrenaline that requires an enemy to maintain its momentum. It moves from the pavement of human effort, fueled by The Group Mind, and it eventually demands a sacrifice to settle the score. In the audit of the flood, justice is merely the redistribution of pain. It tries to heal the world by finding a new person to bleed, unaware that the Father has already closed the ledger at the Cross.

The crowd chose the flood because the river requires rest, and rest feels too dangerous when you have learned that your survival depends on your own momentum. A flood is water out of its proper boundaries, driven by pressure rather than purpose. If you've ever seen a flash flood in a dry canyon, you know the sound: a low, guttural growl that vibrates in your chest before the water even arrives. It's a wall of churning debris that doesn't care about the landscape; it only cares about its own speed.

This happens when our internal counting house goes corporate. It becomes a flood of activity, zeal, and rhetoric that lacks the structural integrity of the Father's heart. In a flood, you lose your footing. You're swept up in the current of the collective roar, shouting for the revolutionary not because you know him, but because the water is moving that way. You surrender your identity as a child of the Father to the safety of the Pack. This is the energy of the pavement, a manic, shared adrenaline that feels like power but is actually the loss of the individual soul to the mass.

Amos and the Cry for Alignment

THIS IS THE CONTEXT FOR ONE OF THE MOST SIGNIFICANT theological pivots in the ancient texts: *But let justice roll on like a river, righteousness like a never-failing stream!* (Amos 5:24).

We often hear this verse as a call for social reform or legal retribution—as if God is demanding a flood of consequences to wash away the sinners. But in the heart of the Father, this is a call for alignment. Amos was speaking to a religious mob obsessed with feasts and the noise of their songs. They were living in a religious flood—lots of activity, but no alignment with the plumb line of the Father.

The thunder Amos heard wasn't God demanding a bigger sacrifice; it was the sound of a Plumb Line dropping into the middle of a chaotic crowd. A plumb line doesn't scream at the wall for being crooked; it simply remains perfectly vertical, providing the silent truth that allows the builder to realign. The plumb line doesn't judge the wall for leaning; it simply offers the wall the truth of its own potential. The Father isn't the Chief of Police breaking up the mob; He is the Master Builder offering the only Line that leads back to rest. He isn't interested in condemning the lean; He is focused on the restoration of the structure.

The River: Water with Boundaries

THE DIFFERENCE BETWEEN A FLOOD AND A RIVER IS THE

bank. The banks are the boundaries of identity. A river is water that knows where it belongs. It has a source, a direction, and a destination. It is water that is indivisibly one with its path. In a river, there is a rhythm—a steady, predictable flow that brings life to everything it touches.

In the Body of Christ, we are called to be a river. While the Mob demands sameness (the Flood), the Body celebrates distinctness (the river). The bank—the Father's secure love—provides the structure so that the water can flow with power without becoming destructive. When we live as a Mob, we use the Scalpel of Exclusion to create artificial banks out of people's behavior. But the Father's restorative justice provides the bank of grace. Grace is the boundary that keeps the river of reconciliation from turning into a destructive flood of religious tribalism. The river doesn't condemn the land it flows through; it nourishes it. It doesn't scream at the rocks in its way; it simply flows around them until they are smooth.

The Reservoir of Narcissism

At the heart of the Corporate Fall is the moment the river stops flowing and becomes a stagnant reservoir. When a community becomes consumed with its own prominence or its own special revelation, it ceases to be a tributary.

The group's mind builds a dam to hoard the water, turning a gift into private property.

Stagnant water doesn't nourish; it breeds. In these 'Reservoirs of the Special,' the air gets heavy with the smell of the Audit. We check water levels—not of grace, but of compliance. Am I still in? Did I say enough amens? Do I still have a seat at the table? This is the mud left behind—the sticky, suffocating residue of a system that promised the Living Water of the Son but delivered the bottled water of a brand.

When a community is healthy, it functions as a tributary. It doesn't draw attention to its own banks; it simply carries the water of the Father's love to the dry places. It follows the Amos mandate: it lets "restoration roll." A river doesn't have to defend itself against the desert; it simply flows until the desert blooms.

The Finishing Current

THE CROSS WAS THE DEFINITIVE ACT THAT BROKE THE dam of the Mob. On the Cross, Jesus absorbed the flood of human rage—the shouting, the spitting, the frantic demand for chaos over peace—and He turned it into the river of life. He took the chaotic noise of the Pavement and answered it with the focused, rhythmic "It is finished" of the Porch.

He allowed the world's transactional justice to execute Him, and in doing so, He proved the river is more powerful than the Flood. He did not retaliate. The roar didn't include him; While the Mob was screaming at its own reflection, the Father was whistling a tune of home that the noise could not drown out.

To walk in this indivisibly one reality, we must have the courage to step away from the Mob. We realize that the statute of limitations has expired on our need to join the roar just to feel safe. The Father is still whistling on the Porch. He isn't calling for a flood; He is calling for a river that doesn't condemn.

The Proximate Weight of Kindness

THIS ISN'T JUST A THEOLOGICAL THEORY FOR ME. IT BE-came the only oxygen available during that painstaking season for our family, when the wreckage of our family's trauma threatened to drown me. In the chapters ahead, we will examine how the river interacts with the most jagged parts of our story—the parts where the world demands a blood-payment that can never be satisfied.

The Father isn't calling for a flash flood of judgment to sweep you away; He is calling for a river that nourishes the very soil of your soul. Step into the current, let the water hit the dry places, and realize that the flow was never against you—it was always for you.

6

The Kiss Of Justice

Amnesty: A legal pardon that clears a record
but does not change a nature. The difference
between being cleared and being reborn.

Atonement and the Porch

THE JOURNEY TO REDEFINE JUSTICE LEADS US INEV-itably to the cross. We have already dismantled the stone walls of the courtroom—the fear, the transaction, and the performance—and replaced them with the warmth of the Father on the Porch. But we must be honest: for many of us, the cross is the very place where the internal courtroom feels most terrifying.

We have received a theology that depicts the crucifixion as divine child abuse, showing a peaceful Son crushed by a furious, blood-hungry Father whose wrath demanded satisfaction.

We've been told that God's justice required a violent payment, and since we couldn't pay it, Jesus had to take the blow.

While the concept of substitution has been the primary lens of the courtroom for centuries, it is often a legal projection that obscures the Father's true heart. When we view the Cross as a mere exchange of one life for another to satisfy a debt, the character we assign to the Father becomes haunting. It portrays Him as a volatile judge who is only safe to be around because He finally drank His fill of vengeance. If the cross is merely a legal execution to satisfy a vengeful debt, then the Porch is a mere daydream. We cannot trust a Father who only loves us because He was paid off.

But the truth is more fierce and more beautiful than a courtroom settlement: the cross is not where the Father expresses His anger; it is where He expresses His ultimate, strategic love. As we saw in the Architecture of Satisfaction, the Cross was not a legal transaction, but the ultimate exposure of the human condition. The Father didn't demand a death to change His mind about us; He allowed a death to change our minds about Him. He wasn't looking for a substitute to hit; He was looking for a way to enter our total collapse and blow the doors off the prison from the inside.

The Scandalous Cross and the Savage Irony

This 'No' was the ultimate exposure of the human condition. While we have often been told the Cross was a legal trans-action to satisfy a Judge, the reality is far more scandalous. We were at our absolute worst—so colonized by the knowledge of good and evil that when Love made flesh walked onto the pavement without a ledger, we tried to extinguish Him.

The crowd got exactly what it asked for. They released the revolutionary and crucified the King. Pilate washed his hands, Barabbas walked free, and Jesus carried His cross through the streets that should have been walked by another. But here is the profound irony, the cosmic reversal that makes the angels weep: In that moment, Jesus didn't just take the place of one man. He occupied the nature of all of us.

In our violent refusal, the Father answered with a reality that was out of all proportion to our rejection. If our worst was capable of attempting to kill Love, the Father's response was a landslide of grace that didn't just cover the offense—it buried the entire geography of the Audit and raised us up in life full tilt. This is the strategic victory: the King used our un-fortunate murder to bankrupt the system of debt and reclaim our nature forever.

Think about what this moment represents. It wasn't just about one person's guilt or innocence. It revealed our tend-ency to choose the sword over the King and the musty base-ment of retribution over the fresh air of reconciliation. This is the gospel in its most shocking form: freedom offered to the guilty, not because a Judge was paid off, but because the King allowed our violence to spend itself on His own heart. It wasn't a cold exchange of blood for debt; it was the total collapse of the prison.

But here's the deeper truth: we who are in Christ walk away from the cross not just pardoned, but transformed. Not just released, but reborn. What happened on that platform wasn't a simple legal exchange; it was a miracle of restoration that raised us up in life full tilt. The blood and water that flowed from Christ's side didn't just balance the world's ledger —it rewrote our very nature.

Born of Opposition: The Mother of Praise

To understand the kiss of justice at the cross, we have to go back to the tribal namesake who paved the way: Judah. We often treat the lineage of Jesus as a flawless, golden chain, but Judah's very first breath was drawn in an atmosphere of bitter, grinding opposition.

Judah was born to Leah—a scorned woman, a wife who was fourth in line for the affection of a man who didn't choose her. The transactional binary defined Leah's existence. She spent years in the low-grade fever of the courtroom, trying to earn her place and win love through the birth of her sons. You can see the progression of her agony in the names she gave her children: *Jehovah has looked upon my affliction, Jehovah has heard that I am hated, Jehovah will join my husband to me.*

She was living for the limelight of her husband's attention, but the middleman of her circumstances kept blocking her way. Then, with her fourth son, something in her spirit shifted. She stopped looking at the empty seat at the table and looked to the God who was already there. Within her pain, she found solid ground and declared, "I will praise Jehovah!"

Judah was born into a lifestyle of praise that didn't emerge from a stage or a spotlight, but from the deliberate sacrifice of a wounded heart. Judah wasn't the 'Seed'—that corner was owned by Abraham, the father of our faith, who believed the Promise before he ever saw a performance. But Judah was the Atmosphere the Seed grew in. He was the first to prove that the indivisibly one reality isn't a reward for a perfect life; it's the roar of a person who has finally stopped trying to earn their way onto the porch. Judah didn't provide the DNA of our salvation; he provided the DNA of our Response.

This resonates deeply with the marrow of my own journey. In a season of intense sifting, loss became more than an event; it became an entity that struck at everything I held in high esteem. During the terrors of that period, when I was at my weakest, I didn't hear a judge's verdict. I heard the words of Emmanuel, "Stay with me." Like Leah, I had to stop striv-

ing for the attention of the religious system—the Hired Hands
—and instead find my worth in the One who was already
standing in the rubble. Judah took his first breath in an atmosphere of worth ascribed, and so must we.

But this understanding of worth ascribed, not earned, is
not just a theological truth—it is a prophetic marking. It is a
calling that requires us to confront the wildness of God's love
and the fierceness of His justice.

The Roar of Origin

My name—Bringer of Truth, God's Messenger—always
felt like a weight I wasn't sure I could carry. I tried to fulfill it
through a gentle handmaiden facade, a religious mask that was
polite, predictable, and entirely too quiet. But the Father
didn't want a handmaiden to manage the wreckage; He
wanted a lioness to confront the lie. I remember a morning in
prayer when the pressure to perform was screaming so loud I
couldn't breathe. I was desperately uttering the Lord's name,
trying to use it as a shield against the anxiety that was dismantling me. At that moment, the atmosphere shifted. I wasn't just
praying; I was being hunted by a love that was more fierce than
my fear. I saw Him—the Lion of Judah. He didn't come to
comfort my gentle side; He charged at me, lifted me by the
jaws, and swallowed me whole.

In that instant, I realized that praise isn't a polite song; it's a predatory roar. It is the sound of the river when it hits a stone wall. Judah's hand is on the neck of his enemies, but I realized my enemy wasn't a person—it was the very system of debt and merit I had been trying to survive. A mandate to govern my life consumed me, not with measures, but with the fierce power of a Daughter who knows a King backed her. This lineage of worth ascribed is a bloodline of the excluded, a family tree of women who refused to stay in the basement. I saw Tamar, whom the system saw as a liability, but the Father saw as righteous because she refused to be erased. I saw Rahab, the prostitute who recognized the flow of the Spirit before the holy people did, and Ruth, the illegal immigrant who broke the banks of the Law with her covenant love. I saw Bathsheba, the living proof that God builds palaces out of the debris of our wreckage. Even Judah, the father of this line, ended his story by offering his own life for his brother. This is the violent heart of the Porch: the ability to preserve a higher worth through sacrifice.

The Painstaking Season and the Arduous Drift

I remember a wild, sun-drenched time when I lived in the throes of bliss. The girl with a tattoo and nose piercing, much to my mother's disapproval, was me. This wasn't due to rebellion, but rather a profound liberation stemming from the joy of a God who truly loved me, a joy I struggled to contain. I knew the shade of the Tree of Life intimately; I lived in the rhythm of the Father's song and savored life's juicy nectar dripping from my chin. But the demand for a verdict often interrupts bliss.

When life ripped at the seams, the music of the Porch became a faint echo. In the first chapter, I showed you the clinical shards of the story—the courtroom facts and the legal briefs—but here is the weight of the wreckage that the law couldn't touch. The first domino fell in a silence that still haunts me: the discovery that a family member had been grooming our daughters. That violation set off a chain reaction that spared nothing. Our church community fractured, friends drifted away, my husband faced a lawsuit, and our youngest son was diagnosed with Type 1 Diabetes. This relentless, hourly battle appeared to mirror the trauma we were already breathing.

I didn't trade the Porch for the Courtroom in a single moment; it was a slow, arduous drift. I moved from the laughter of the Porch to the white-knuckled defense of the courtroom —not because I wanted to leave the Father, but because I felt I had to manage the truth He seemed unwilling to enforce. Because I no longer felt safe enough, I managed the grace instead of simply resting in it. The breach left me questioning everything I thought I knew about justice, grace, and the

Father's love. I was exhausted, trying to hold the seams together while the music of the Porch grew distant, unaware that even beneath the rubble of my management, the river was still carving a way forward.

The Torrent

I realize that speaking of violence and fierceness might feel like a gearshift away from the quiet river we've been swimming in. In previous chapters, I told you that God's justice is not a destructive flash flood. So how do I reconcile that with a personal prophecy I received, where the Lord called me a torrent and a violent rushing stream? The distinction lies in the flow's target. The violence of the Kingdom is not directed at the person; it is directed at the obstacles—the religious systems, the Late-Night Audits, and the predatory lies that keep us from the Father.

The Old System uses the flood to destroy the person. It weaponized shame, guilt, and fear to crush the individual under its weight. But the river of reconciliation is a torrent that destroys the lie. It is only quiet to those it is carrying; to the obstacles in its way—the religious systems, the groomers, the vultures—it is a devastating force. The Father's love is gentle toward the child, but it is a maternal torrent toward the shame that tries to enslave that child.

A season arrived when I retreated from the wild wind that

authored me. The searing loss I carried had shaped me in ways I didn't recognize. I dressed myself up—soul and body—in an attempt to cover the pain, to present a version of motherhood that felt more manageable, more acceptable. I tried to be meek and mild, a gentle handmaiden who wouldn't disrupt the waters.

But God didn't mince words when He came to strip away the costume. He shattered the facade I had cloaked myself in and made a brutal declaration, "You are my violent one!" He reached into my nature and said: 'You are the biological daughter of a violent man and the original daughter of the King of Kings, who will violently protect what He spoke into existence.' Within that declaration was a message: I was born of intensity, both in flesh and spirit, but God was reclaiming it. He wasn't making me angry; He was transforming my wounds into relentless warfare.

This echoed a word the Lord had spoken over me: "She's the torrent, the wicked dread and the sweet rapture that the lost ones hope for." To the lost one, I am a rapture of relief—a rushing stream that carries them to safety. But to the performer who fronts and peacocks in his own strength, I am a flood that reduces his religious wineskins to rubble.

This fierce, restorative love is not a contradiction to God's justice—it is the very definition of it. To understand this, we must explore the paradox of the Cross, where God is both Just and the Justifier.

The Paradox of the Just and the Justifier

At the intellectual heart of this kiss lies the paradox of Romans 3:26: *...it was to show his righteousness at the present time, so that he might be just and the justifier of the one who has faith in Jesus.* This wasn't just a theological theory for me; it was the only thing that kept me from drowning during the seasons when I was forced to maintain the facade of the porch. I had to know that God wasn't just nice, I had to know He was Just, and that His justice was big enough to handle the violation I was touching.

I have witnessed the fallout of a theology that views the Father as a Judge who was pleased to strike His Son. When people believe the Cross was an act of divine retribution, they eventually use that belief as permission to strike others down in the same way. They mirror a God they've cast in the image of a legalist, who believes that justice only satisfies when someone adheres to their understanding of truth, even if it means suffering. But that is the logic of the counting house, not of the river.

In the original Greek, to be just (*dikaios*) does not mean to be punitive; it means to be balanced, right, and true to one's original design. It means God is just because He refuses to let a lie—whether your sin or the wreckage others have caused—define the truth of who you are. He is the Justifier because He is the one who restores that balance. He doesn't justify the crime; He justifies the person by pulling them out of the wreckage and back to the Porch.

The Father remains just because He upholds His standard of wholeness. His justice is not about retribution; it is about restoration. He is true to His nature as a Restorer, always working to bring creation back into alignment with His original design. He is the Justifier because He is the one who declares the true nature over you: You are a New Creation. This was not a cosmic conflict between an angry Father and a pleading Son. The Father was in Christ (2 Corinthians 5:19), fully taking part in the swallowing up of merit-based living and reconciling the world to himself. The Cross does not represent the moment the Father's wrath was satisfied; it's the moment the Lion of Judah consumed the courtroom.

The Cross is the ultimate paradox: justice and mercy, judgment and grace, the ledger and the river, all converging in one act of self-giving love. The Father revealed his justice in this moment, not as punishment, but as the relentless pursuit of wholeness. This pursuit of wholeness is not just theological; it is deeply practical. Nowhere is this more clear than in the way Jesus dealt with shame on the cross.

Scorning the Shame: Breaking the Groomer's Tool

The author of Hebrews tells us that Jesus *endured the cross, scorning its shame* (Hebrews 12:2). This is where hand-holding gets practical. Religion often uses shame as its primary currency. I constantly audited myself, as they told me I wasn't 'pure enough' or that I didn't yet have the right 'calling' or 'anointing.' This is spiritual grooming—the use of authority, approval, and subtle manipulation to keep you small, compliant, and dependent. It's a system designed to make you question your worth and tether your identity to the validation of others.

But on the cross, Jesus didn't just take our sins; He took the world's system of shame. By dying naked and mocked, He exhausted the power of the auditor. He wore the labels—sinner, rejected, unclean—into the grave and left them there. The cross is the ultimate declaration that shame has no authority over you. If the Son of God embraced the ultimate shame of the cross, then you and I are forever freed from the power of human peacocking. The need to perform, the constant auditing, the labels—they hold no weight in the presence of One who scorned shame itself. This is the breaking of the groomer's tool: the realization that your worth is not up for debate. The Father gives it, the Son confirms it, and the river transmits it.

And this breaking of shame is not just a personal victory; it is a royal declaration. The cross, which the world saw as a place of humiliation, was in fact the throne room of the King.

The Coronation on Calvary: The Throne of Wood

The world saw the Cross as a place of ultimate humiliation —the final verdict of the accounts. But for the Father, Calvary was the throne room. In John's Gospel, the scene is dripping with kingly irony. The soldiers gambled for His seamless robe —the garment of a High Priest. Pilate writes the title 'King of the Jews' in three languages, unwittingly proclaiming a truth far greater than he understood. The crown of thorns, meant to mock, became a symbol of His eternal kingship.

It looked like defeat, but it was a coronation. The Father didn't ask His Son to die to satisfy a personal need for violence; He crowned Him with the authority to dismantle the entire transactional system. The Cross is the moment the Lamb Slain claimed His eternal dominion. It is the throne of wood where the King of Kings issued His royal decree: The accounting house is permanently closed. The river is permanently open.

This coronation was not just a moment of irony; it was the fulfillment of a Kingdom that operates on entirely different terms. The ledger demanded payment, yet the river flows freely. While math measures worth, it is the river that declares it. The audit kept humanity in a cycle of shame and striving, but the river invites us to rest in the finished work of the King. The Cross is the ultimate paradox: a place of suffering that became the seat of victory, a moment of humiliation that became the declaration of glory. It is the throne of wood where justice and mercy kissed, and the King of Kings declared His eternal reign. And now, the river flows from that throne, carrying the invitation to rest in what has already been accomplished.

The Unlocked City: The Gates That Never Close

The entire journey of this book culminates in this kiss. It is the scene described in Psalm 85:10: *Mercy and truth have met together; righteousness and peace have kissed each other*. At the Cross, they embrace. The Truth of your eternal value and the Mercy that swallows your wreckage met and kissed, dissolving the courtroom in that embrace.

John the Revelator, standing at the end of all things, gives us the ultimate picture of this restorative reality. In his vision of the Holy City, the New Jerusalem, John the Revelator makes a staggering declaration: *On no day will its gates ever be shut, for there will be no night there* (Revelation 21:25). Gates were closed at night out of fear—fear of the predator, fear of the invader. To close a gate is to announce a state of siege, to declare that danger is near. But in the reality of the Finished Work, the Light of the Lamb has extinguished the night of the soul. The predators of shame and the invaders of religion have no power here.

The Father has not only invited you to the Porch; He has removed the very possibility of your exclusion. There is no lock on the door, no guard at the threshold, no conditions to meet. The Kiss of Justice didn't just settle a case; it unlocked a Kingdom. But here's the challenge: while the Father's gates are forever open, we often keep our own gates closed. Our errant theology of distance serves as the justification for the walls we erect, effectively barring others while imprisoning ourselves. We cling to the transactional pursuit, measuring who is worthy of our love, our forgiveness, our trust. We post keep out signs on the gates of our hearts, convinced that distance offers us permission to reject others.

This is the lie of the Old System: that separation is safety, that exclusion is justice, that distance is holiness. But the truth of the open gates is this: the glory that will cover the whole earth like the waters cover the seas will spill out through our open gates. The river flows through us, and it cannot flow if we keep the gates shut. When we live under the truth of open gates, we become the conduits of the Father's heart. The invitation of the Porch extends through us to all men. When we refuse to participate in their systems, the predators of shame and the invaders of religion lose their power. The distance dissolves, and the Kingdom advances—not by coercion, but through the relentless, uncontainable flow of the river—a force that dismantles lies and lays hold of truth.

It's a wrap on the audition. The gates are open. The Father is whistling, and He's not planning on coming inside anytime soon. He's staying on the Porch, watching the horizon, because He knows that in a city where the gates never close, there is nothing left to keep you from Him, or to keep you from others. The gates that never close are the ultimate expression of the Father's heart.

The Porch is not just a place of invitation—it is the very foundation of a Kingdom where exclusion is impossible, and love is the only law. The kiss of justice didn't just settle a case; it unlocked a Kingdom. It proved that the Father's Yes is the only floor that holds, and it raises us up in life full tilt—moving us from the siege of the gate to the freedom of the Porch.

So step through the gates. Let the river carry you. Open your own gates to the world around you. Rest in the Kiss's embrace and let the glory spill out. You are no longer a defendant awaiting a verdict; you are a child of the landslide, and the restoration is in progress.

The Father is waiting, and the gates will never close.

Before we move forward, I want to pause here. If you've ever found yourself in a breach of your own—where the seams of life have torn apart and the music of the Porch feels distant —I invite you to sit with me for a moment. Let's acknowledge the weight of the wreckage, the ache of unanswered questions, and the exhaustion of trying to hold it all together. But as we sit here, let's also remember: the river is still flowing. Even when it feels hidden beneath the rubble, it is carving a way forward. This carving is not always gentle. Sometimes the river becomes a torrent—a violent rushing stream that destroys the lies in its way.

7

The Disarmed Shadow

Why the Body Still Trembles in a Disarmed World

I F THE GATES ARE NEVER TO BE CLOSED AGAIN, AS John declared, then the question for the heart changes from, "How do I get in?" to "How do I live now that I am here?" We have spent so long scratching at the door of the courtroom that the wide-open threshold of the Father's house can feel disorienting. Like released prisoners, we still walk in the tight, circular patterns of our former cells. We aren't looking for the door anymore; we are looking for the catch.

The Great Exchange was the legal and foundational reality, but abiding is the rhythmic reality. It is where the indivisibly one nature we received at the Cross breathes through our hands, our words, and our quietest thoughts. To move from the pavement to the Porch is to trade the frantic pace of the mob for the steady, unhurried flow of the river.

There is a staggering gap between the finished work of the Cross and the unfinished feeling in our nervous systems. We know, intellectually, that the war is over. We have established our home on the Porch. Yet, the moment we attempt to relax into that embrace, a tripwire is often triggered. This feverish anxiety is not always a theological misunderstanding; it is an architectural legacy. It is the way our bodies have been hard-wired to survive a courtroom that no longer has any legal jurisdiction over us. To live from our restored original design, we must first understand why the shadow still feels so substantial and why our bodies continue to brace for a blow that is never coming. The mind may accept the Father's verdict of being justified, but the nervous system is a different witness. Even after we've settled our emotional debt, our nervous system retains proof of our pain, expecting more trouble to arise—or in my case, awaiting the impact of a knee on a shin.

We often treat this residual anxiety as a spiritual failure—a sign that we don't have enough faith or that we haven't mastered the Gospel yet. But I see that our Biology is actually a profound theological witness. The Father did not make a mistake when He gave us a nervous system. He didn't slip up when He installed the amygdala—that primitive, unblinking smoke detector in the brain's basement.

Our bodies were designed for Union's unhurried oxygen. Long before we ever drew our first breath on this side of the veil, our cells were curated in the warmth of the Father's hands. Jeremiah speaks of a God who knew us before He ever formed us in the womb, and the Psalmist describes a Father who knit us together in the secret place. That thought offers incredible tenderness: an assembly line did not manufacture us;; we were hand-stitched. If we were knit together by the hands of Love, then our very fibers have a cellular memory of that original touch.

Our Biology is an honest historian. It doesn't just remember the metallic chill of the courtroom; it remembers the proximal heat of One who knit the stitches. It remembers being held long before we were ever measured. Therefore, when we try to survive in the musty basement of the Audit, our Biology does exactly what it was designed to do: it complains. The fever of anxiety isn't a glitch; it's a biological homesickness—a violent protest by a body that remembers being held and refuses to 'make nice' with an environment of performance.

The amygdala sounds the alarm, signaling that we are breathing the toxic fumes of separation when we were built for the fresh air of the Porch, making the shadow feel so substantial. It is the knitting holding the standard, refusing to settle for anything less than the original embrace.

The Pebble in the Gears

I WAS IN THE GYM FOR BASKETBALL PRACTICE, PLAYING on the scrimmage team. Physically, I felt fine—at least, that's what I told myself. In the third quarter, I was holding a tight zone defense when a point guard plowed through the lane. Her knee drove hard into my leg, just below the joint. It was a standard athletic injury, the kind I had walked off a hundred times before. I limped it out, but as soon as I saw the massive, throbbing bump forming on my shin, my body fainted.

My vision tunneled into grey static. The squeak of sneakers and the rhythmic thud of the ball receded into a distant, metallic hum. I collapsed. When I regained consciousness, the head coach, also a nurse, loomed over me with a look that suggested the ER awaited me. My daughter stood beside him, and her wide eyes conveyed her terror, as she thought I was broken. I truthfully felt broken as well, because my body reacted nonsensically. A bruised knee does not cause a total system blackout.

My body had executed its ultimate safe-mode: Dorsal Vagal Shutdown. It was a clinical circuit-breaker—my brain's alarm system, the amygdala, realized the system could not process one more ounce of sensory data after a year of redlining in the Audit. A bruised knee didn't break me; it just provided the pebble that caused the engine to stall.

The Mechanics of the Stall

TO UNDERSTAND WHY A BRUISED KNEE TRIGGERED A total system blackout, you have to look past the hardwood of the basketball court and into the redlining mechanics of my internal engine.

Before that moment in the gym, there had been a decade of structural strain. I had spent years standing in the yard of my life with my arms spread wide, desperately holding grace as a shield while trying to keep the chaos from consuming my family. I wasn't sure how long we could keep up with the push and pull dynamics of a heart that sought relief in distance and my own desperate need for order. My theology told me I was on the Porch, but my Biology still convinced me I was a defendant in the Courtroom.

Then came the hellish year. Only months before that basketball practice, the discovery of the predator in our midst had shattered our world. For twelve months, my foot had pressed the pedal to the floor. Imagine a high-performance engine designed for the long haul. Under normal circumstances, it purrs at a steady RPM. But my engine stayed in the red zone for a solid year.

My nervous system was running at 8,000 RPMs just to keep the house from vibrating apart. I was functioning in a state of hyper-vigilance, where every phone call or knock at the door was a potential site for a new trauma. This is the exhaustion of the audit—a high-voltage existence that assumes a blow is always coming.

Even with the chains of religious performance gone, the mechanical reality was that my biological oil was thinning and my temperature gauge was in the danger zone. The danger of coming out of deep darkness is that we lose our baseline for normal. I mistook the adrenaline of survival for the oxytocin of peace. It didn't occur to me that my better was still 7,000 RPMs higher than my body could maintain. I was sprinting on a broken soul and calling it progress.

When that point guard's knee hit my leg, it wasn't a head-on collision; it was just a pebble. But when an engine is red-lining for that long, it doesn't take a wreck to cause a stall. It only takes a pebble in the gears to trigger a dorsal vagal shut-down. My body didn't fail; it just finally executed its safe mode.

The Mercy of the Stall

This is where the mechanical meets the theological. We often view a stall as a failure of the machine, but in the hands of a master mechanic, a stall is a design feature. It is a mercy.

In the courtroom, a stall is a liability—it is contempt of court. In the Audit's world, if you stop performing, you lose your standing. But the Porch is the only jurisdiction where hitting zero is not a bankruptcy, but a prerequisite for the feast.

I had spent a lifetime trying to balance the measures of Strength. I believed that as long as I could keep the engine running; I was winning. But the Father knows that a redlining engine eventually melts. If my body hadn't forced me to the sidelines that day, I would have burned out the very parts of me meant for the Porch.

The stall was God's way of overriding the mask I wore. It was the moment the plumb line of my humanity hit the floor. In the silence of that blackout, the Father wasn't auditing my performance; He was cooling my engine. He allowed my strength to hit zero so that I could finally recognize that my survival didn't depend on my RPMs, but on His presence.

He was teaching me that the Porch is not a place for high-performance engines; it is a place for children who know they are held. The stall wasn't a punishment for being weak; it was an invitation to stop pretending I was strong.

A Neurological Relic: Body Memory

OUR BODIES ARE THE HISTORIANS OF OUR TRAUMA. While our spirits are the recipients of a new nature, our nervous systems often lag behind the news. I know this architecture intimately. Even now, after walking onto the Porch, I deal with the residual effects of a decade spent neck-deep in a religious system that functioned as a plantation of performance. During those years, my body was not a sanctuary; it was a radar dish, constantly scanning for the next strike of the gavel.

The shadow is the neurological pathway created by years of shadowboxing a life I thought was failing me. When we lived under the weight of legalism, we were in a constant state of sympathetic nervous system activation—the fight or flight response. Your body trained itself to see safety as a trap and quiet as the pause before punishment.

Consider the metaphor of a long-term prisoner. After thirty years in a six-by-nine-foot cell, the guards finally threw open the gates. He is legally free to walk into the sunlight. They provide him a suite in a five-star hotel with a plush mattress and a view of the ocean. But that night, the maid finds him sleeping on the cold, hard floor of the bathroom.

He is not being rebellious; he is being mechanical. His body does not know how to handle the lack of resistance. To his nervous system, the bars were the only thing that gave him a sense of where he was. The safety of the hotel feels like a threat because he has not yet developed the posture of a free man.

This is the distinction between your Ontology and your Biology. Your Ontology is the finished reality of your nature. In Christ, you already possess a seated position, wholeness, and unassailability. You are the man in the five-star hotel. Your

Biology, however, is the neurological relic, the physical historian that is still catching up to the news of your freedom.

You are not fighting a spiritual war for your identity; you are undergoing a biological renovation of your nervous system.

This is the state of many believers. We have been legally evicted from the Courtroom, but we are spiritually squatting in our old cell because the Porch feels too good to be true. We have an addiction to the struggle's security. The shadow isn't a sign of a failed nature; it's just the dust rising as the Father remodels the house. Our bodies are still standing on Pilate's pavement, braced for the verdict.

We have been told for so long that we are one mistake away from crucifixion that our nervous systems cannot quite believe we got the Barabbas deal—that someone else took the blow, and we walked away free. The shadow is not a sign that the exchange did not work; it is just the body's slow realization that the platform is empty and the cross is behind us.

The Iniquity of the Fathers: Genetic Architecture

A QUESTION THAT OFTEN HAUNTS THOSE STANDING IN the in-between is the reality of generational patterns. We see the same sins, the same addictions, and the same specific brand of fear echoing down through three or four generations like a persistent, unwanted ghost. The math of merit often preaches this as a legal curse, a divine judgment requiring us to litigate our way back into God's good graces.

But through the lens of the river, we see that iniquity is not a legal sentence; it is an architectural inheritance.

Iniquity, in its original Hebrew sense (*'āwōn*), refers to a 'bending' or a 'distortion' of the path. It is a warp in the floorboards of the family home. When a father spends his life shadowboxing the Audit, he doesn't just produce a theology; he builds a courtroom atmosphere in his house. His children inhale his nervous system. They learned the rhythm of the counting. They don't just hear his words; they absorb the tension in his shoulders and the heavy, metallic tone of his silence.

This is the visiting of iniquity. It is the transmission of a distorted architecture. The third and fourth generation is not a limit on God's anger; it is the natural reach of a human life's influence. A man's group mind typically touches his grandchildren and his great-grandchildren. He passes down the blueprint of the shadow, and unless someone realizes the gates are open, the children will continue to sleep on the cold floor of that old cell because that is the only floor they've ever known. They repeat the father's sins not because they are cursed, but because no one ever showed them where the light switch was.

This truth reframes our responsibility. The cycle is not

broken by casting out a demon of inheritance, but by consciously choosing to build a new home on the foundation of the Porch. We tear up the warped floorboards by living in the reality of the river. We teach the next generation a new rhythm —the unhurried, steady cadence of grace. By resting in the Father's love, we rewire not only our own nervous systems but provide a new blueprint for those who come after us, showing them that the light has been on all along.

The statute of limitations on your family's baggage has not just expired; the entire case has been dismissed because the nature that carried the baggage has been replaced. You are no longer the product of your past; you are the product of His promise. Justice declared its verdict, and it finished its pronouncement over your bloodline.

The Bloodline vs. The Nature: The Final Verdict on the Tree

WHEN WE TALK ABOUT THE INIQUITY OF THE FATHERS, we must realize that Justice has already had the ultimate word. In the old courtroom, the enemy used your family tree as a weapon of accusation, pointing to the patterns of the past as proof of your future. He would trace the tangled roots of addiction, anxiety, and failure, claiming they were the inevitable fruit of your lineage. But the Kiss of Justice at the Cross was a retroactive decree. It did not just stop the clock on your sins; it reset the clock on your entire heritage.

If Justice is the plumb line of the Father's heart, then the final verdict on your family tree is restoration. The Father is not looking back at your third and fourth generations to find a reason to limit your inheritance. He is visiting the tree to plant the river. He is the God who makes all things new, and this renewal includes the very soil where your nervous system grows. Where the enemy sees a curse to be managed, the Father sees a root system ready to be redeemed.

You are no longer grafting your life into a dying tree, trying to squeeze sustenance from dry branches. You are rooted in the Vine that has already conquered the drought. The sap flowing through your veins is no longer the old man's survival instinct; it is the new man's abundant life. The generational cycle is broken not by your effort to be better than your father, but by your acceptance that you have a new Father altogether. The bloodline of Adam has been superseded by the bloodline of the Son, and in this new lineage, there are no warped floorboards—only the solid, unshakable ground of grace.

The Anatomy of a Religious Trigger

A RELIGIOUS TRIGGER IS A FLASHBACK OF THE NERVOUS system. When we spend years on the plantation of performance, we aren't just learning theology; we are being conditioned. This often manifests in the specific vibe of an environment—the weeping tone of a worship leader or the hushed, manipulative gravity of a certain prayer.

Your chest tightens not because the Holy Spirit is convicting you, but because your brain remembers the Mud Vats of trying to conjure a feeling to prove you were spiritual enough to belong.

These triggers are the echoes of a system that taught us to equate emotional intensity with spiritual sincerity. We learned to perform our repentance, our worship, and our devotion, hoping that if we looked the part, we might eventually feel it. The problem is that this kind of striving does not produce the peace of the Porch; it creates a state of high alert.

Our bodies learned to associate the sacred with the stressful. The sanctuary became a stage, and our worship became an audition. When you encounter those old cues—a specific chord progression or a phrase heavy with religious jargon—your body doesn't hear an invitation; it hears a summons back to the Courtroom.

Healing begins with the radical act of giving our bodies permission to feel safe. We must call it what it is: Religious PTSD. The shadow's architecture tries to protect you from a threat that no longer poses danger.

The Grapple in the Living Room

THE ARCHITECTURE OF THE COURTROOM ISN'T JUST A theory; it is a physical sensation. I felt this architecture flare to life in a living room during a gathering of leaders. I was sitting in a circle when the atmosphere shifted into a technical coldness. A leader addressed the room in the third person, speaking about me as if I were an absent object of study.

In an instant, my anatomy eclipsed my fundamental peace. A physical fire rose through my chest. My heart rate spiked, and my mind automatically scanned for a survival strategy to mitigate the public shaming. I found myself in a grapple: one foot remained on the Porch, anchored in the truth of my belonging, while the other wandered into the old territory of self-protection.

In the heat of that trigger, the Holy Spirit didn't shame my wandering foot. He didn't demand a precision of surrender. Instead, He coached me through the anatomy of the audit: "Angie, own it. Respond with a humble heart and own it."

I didn't hide. The room was addressed directly by me. I said, 'That was me.' And then I asked the defining question: 'Why had you not said this to me in real-time?' That is the practical reality of scorning the shame. It isn't a loud, defensive posture; it is a quiet, resolute refusal to let your anatomy dictate your identity. By owning the story, auditing power is disempowered. You stop being a defendant and start being a Daughter who simply refuses to leave the table.

The Sovereign Mandate: Rewiring the Sanctuary

Dismantling this architecture requires the authority of an heir who knows the disarmed enemy thrives on these neurological relics. He plays the old soundtrack of the courtroom through the speakers of your nervous system, hoping you will be too distracted by the noise to enjoy the feast. But the shadow is not a sign that the kiss of justice did not work; it is simply a sign that you are a human being with a history. Your trembling does not embarrass the Father; it moves Him.

To break this cycle, we must learn to interrupt the loop. When a trigger pulls, we can stop and acknowledge it as a mechanical echo rather than a spiritual reality. We tell ourselves, 'My body is reacting to an old lie, but I am safe. This is a shadow, not a courtroom.' By identifying the biological nature of the anxiety, we strip it of its religious authority and allow our nervous system to return to its proper RPMs. We take the remote back from the ghost of the plantation.

Next, we must saturate the senses with the current reality of the Porch. Reminders of the Father's unhurried love will take the place of triggers. We find God in the rain's scent, the sound of laughter, or the voices of those whose tone carries the fresh air of reconciliation. Rather than seeking Him in the sorrowful sounds of the plantation, we begin to perceive Him in the uncomplicated, constant beat of our transformed existence. We have to train our eyes to see the gates that never close rather than the bars that used to be there.

Finally, we must embrace the grace of time. You cannot rush the renovation of your body's learned responses. The legal victory was instant, but the rewiring of your brain is a process of abiding. The architecture of the shadow is a relic, and it takes time to move your bed from the cell floor to the porch. You are not failing to achieve peace; you are learning the language of a country you were always meant to live in. We do not permit the tremble to become a lifestyle; we recognize it as a signal that we have momentarily drifted back toward the Scales—and then we walk back to the river.

The architecture of the shadow is crumbling. It cannot stand in the Porch's light. Every time you choose to tune your ears to the Father's whistle—that low, steady frequency of "It is finished"—over the frantic, high-pitched alarm of the amygdala, you are tearing down a stone of the old courtroom.

You are choosing to believe a sound that is unhurried and calm over a biological echo that is desperate and loud. In doing so, you aren't just coming home in spirit; you are retraining every fiber of your being to recognize the soundtrack of Home.

Evicting the Squatter

The question turn toward home? is the single, crucial query presented to every soul that recognizes the exhaustion of striving. It is the moment the Older Brother must decide to leave his systems of works, drop his legal brief, and run into the embrace of the Father on the Porch.

But let's be honest: this decision, though simple in relationship, is terrifying in a world that feels rigged for pain. We have been conditioned to believe that the moment we stop working, the protection stops. The spiritual air around us feels heavy with the threat of consequence, and every misstep sounds like the gavel of condemnation echoing through the hallways of our minds. We fear that releasing our grip and turning homeward will leave us vulnerable to a cosmic crossfire. We worry that grace is too thin a shield for the battles we face.

Therefore the Kiss of Justice was necessary. Christ's triumphant act was not just a beautiful theological concept; it was a cosmic intervention that secured the path of return, making the turn toward home safe, legal, and unhindered. He did not just clear the path; He removed the one who was standing in the way.

The enemy of our souls has long operated as a squatter on the territory of our peace. He has no deed, no title, and no right to be there, yet he occupies the space through the power of suggestion and the weapon of memory. He convinces us that the courtroom is still in session and that he is still the prosecutor. But the Cross served him with an eviction notice that cannot be appealed.

Evicting the squatter is to finally agree with the legal reality of the Kingdom. You confront the fear that says, 'You are not safe,' by responding with the truth, 'You are trespassing.' When we turn toward home, we are not walking into a trap; we are walking into a space that has been swept clean of every accusation. The only thing waiting for us on the Porch is the Father, who isn't checking a ledger but is simply watching the road, ready to run.

The Hijacked Cathedral: The Geography of the Lie

THE GYMNASIUM WAS TYPICALLY MY HAPPY PLACE. I loved the physics of it—the sharp, staccato chirp of sneakers on the high-gloss court. But starting in second grade, they hijacked that sanctuary. The D.A.R.E. program arrived like a spiritual audit before I even knew how to balance a checkbook. I can still hear the metallic jingle of the officers' handcuffs and the heavy thud of their boots as they paced the stage, turning the hardwood where I practiced layups into a backdrop for a lecture on moral failure and the inevitable fall.

Hundreds of us would march into the all-school assembly, sitting cross-legged on the polished floor, the air thick with the scent of leftover lunch and the nervous energy of children. When the officers entered, the booming, amplified voices of the Law replaced the echo of the bouncing balls. My sanctuary was officially a courtroom.

The Officers stood at the front of the room, a study in legality. They wore full uniforms: pressed, dark, and imposing. I can still hear the metallic jingle of their handcuffs and the heavy thud of their boots as they paced the stage. Every time the light glinted off the barrel of a holstered gun, I'd hold my breath. The juxtaposition was jarring: the net where I practiced my layups was now the backdrop for a lecture on moral failure and the inevitable fall.

The officer, a man who seemed ten feet tall from my vantage point on the floor, was not a coach encouraging us to run faster; he was a prosecutor warning us about a darkness he assumed we didn't know yet. He spoke of addiction, prison, and death with a terrifying certainty. The message was binary and brutal: there is a narrow line of 'good,' and one misstep sends you into the darkness forever.

I would wiggle, repositioning my small body, trying to find

a spot on that hardwood floor where the fraudulence did not feel so heavy. Proximity is a strange thing. For most kids, home is where they go to escape the school's audit. But because I lived directly across the street, there was no transition—only a narrow strip of asphalt separating the 'Sanctuary of Law' from the 'Plantation of Secret.' I looked at the Just Say No posters in the hallways and didn't see a message of help; I saw a conviction.

While the officers paced the front of the room, I thought of the drugs tucked under the furniture in my own living room—the hidden baggage of a home life that stood in stark contrast to the voices echoing off the walls of my beleaguered heart. I was a child living in a profound duality, a second-grade defendant who knew that if I spoke the truth about the mess across the street, I would be betraying the only sanctuary I had.

My theology would be impacted for decades by a lesson I learned that day: One finds safety not in their identity, but in their adherence to rules. I learned to walk softly, to scan the horizon, and to wait for the floor to drop out. These officers weren't just teachers; they were the first Hired Hands I ever met. They didn't come to offer the river; they came to install the Audit. As they paced, the jingle of their handcuffs provided the rhythm for a gospel of consequence—a message that bad was a destination we were all one mistake away from visiting.

For the entirety of my elementary career, I remained in that docket. The officers did a fine job, but they didn't just teach me to resist drugs; they accidentally taught my nervous system to resist peace. They gave me the tools to avoid a substance, but they stripped me of the capacity to recognize a Sanctuary.

The Great Divestment

The moment righteousness and Peace kissed on the cross, the entire structure of the fallen world's spiritual governance collapsed. The legal, transactional system that demanded death and enforced consequences lost its authority.

The Apostle Paul affirms this as the historical reality of the Cross: Christ *disarmed the principalities and powers, triumphing over them by the cross* (Colossians 2:15). The word translated as disarmed is *apekdyomai*. It literally means to strip off, to divest, to render utterly naked. At the cross, Christ didn't just defeat the enemy; He stripped him of his uniform, his weapons, and his authority, parading him through the streets of the cosmos as a defeated fraud. He publicly exposed the enemy's rule as illegitimate. The transactional system is, simply, bankrupt. God absorbed the debt into His body, and they fired the debt collector.

When Christ disarmed the principalities and powers, He was doing publicly what Barabbas never could. The revolutionary tried to defeat Rome with a sword; he only fed the cycle of violence and retribution. Jesus defeated the entire spiritual empire behind Rome by refusing to play by the Audit. He let them crucify Him, and in that act of supreme vulnerability, He shattered the system that runs on power and fear.

Barabbas walked away from the platform carrying his sword, still bound to the logic of retribution. He was free, but his mind was likely still that of a prisoner of war, ready for the next fight. We, however, walk away from the cross carrying nothing but the knowledge that the enemy is already paraded, already mocked, already defeated. The squatter has been legally evicted. The only fight left is the one for our own belief—the struggle to accept that the war is truly over and that we are safe.

The Irony of the Crack

THE ULTIMATE GOD-HUMOR LIES IN THE FACT THAT DECades later, the Father sat at a desk in the dark and bypassed that childhood police officer by using the very language I was trained to fear.

We had just finished dinner, and everyone had scattered

from the dining room. I retreated to the desk in a quiet corner, facing the hand-printed sliding glass door. The light of the computer monitor guided me to the teaching I had been aching to hear. I have a predisposition to reject drug references; they typically cause my body to recoil from the moment. I was still that little girl terrified of the D.A.R.E. assembly.

But when the speaker said, 'The Cross is the Crack of Heaven,' he was not just using a drug reference; he was breaking the D.A.R.E. seal on my heart. In that instant, the phrase that should have triggered a full-body alarm instead became a key. It was a divine hijacking of a hijacked memory. The statement bypassed the internal officer completely and addressed the prisoner he was guarding. It told me that the police were no longer at the door. When the Father whispered the Cross was the 'Crack of Heaven,' He was doing more than using a drug reference to heal a trauma. He was performing a Sovereign Reclaim. He was reaching back to that second-grade girl sitting cross-legged on the floor and telling her that the 'Hijacked Cathedral' was His all along. The floor wasn't for auditing; it was for dancing. The officers had been evicted, and the Father had moved in across the street.

The fraudulent feeling I had carried since second grade dissolved. The Father had already moved in across the street. Something magnificent was happening. I felt as if the city on the inside of me had lit up, every streetlamp and window glowing at once. The circuit was finally closing. My chest felt like an open horizon, lit by a thousand streetlamps at once.

The Cross did not just crack the floor; it cleared the room. It took down the posters, folded up the heavy lunchroom tables, and threw the ball back to me. It was as if the Father leaned in and whispered, 'Angie, the street is gone. There is no 'across.' You are home, and you may play.' The most addictive, life-altering substance in the universe is not something to be feared but the very thing that sets us free. The irony was that it was healing. Conditioning made me run from the language of my homecoming.

The Ghost in the Machine: Why the Echo Persists

WHY DOES THIS HAPPEN IF THEY STRIP THE ENEMY AND parade the General naked? The air still feels charged with a fight. This is where many get stuck. We assume that if we achieve victory, the symptoms should vanish instantly.

But there is a profound difference between a legal reality and a neurological habit. This ghost is not a demon to be fought, but a neurological relic to be healed. It is the echo of old adrenaline loops that haven't yet realized the war is over.

When we live in the courtroom, our brains process information like accountants. We have what has been called 'The

Ghost in the Machine'—a residual survival instinct that keeps looking for a threat even though the threat no longer exists. This is the source of that low-grade fever of anxiety we carry. Even when the Father is singing a lullaby, our internal Older Brother is pacing the floor, scanning the horizon for the tax man.

The enemy knows this. He is disarmed, yes, but he is also a master of leverage. Convincing you that your own shadow is an assassin negates his need for a sword. He relies on the fact that religion has groomed you to expect a blow. He operates like a squatter who legally owns the house but an eviction occurred. Although he knows he has no right to the property; he's hoping that by making enough noise, rattling the pipes, and casting scary shadows on the wall, you'll be too terrified to claim the keys.

This ghost is not a spirit you need to cast out; it is a memory you need to heal. It is the echo of old adrenaline loops that haven't yet realized the war is over. When your heart races or your stomach knots up in a church service, it isn't necessarily a demon attacking you; it is often just your amygdala doing what it was trained to do in the presence of performance-based religion.

Recognizing the ghost for what it is—an echo, not an entity—changes the way we fight. We stop swinging swords in the air and start speaking peace to our own Biology. We stop rebuking the darkness and start turning on the light. The squatter has no power other than the power of suggestion. The fear loses its power the moment you understand you can unplug from the machine causing the noise. You can stand in the middle of the noise, hold up the deed to your heart signed in the blood of the Son, and politely but firmly tell the ghost that the Master of the house has come home.

The Tactics of the Disarmed: Deception and Fear

THE JURISDICTION OF THE COSMOS HAS BEEN ETERNALLY settled, and the battle has now entirely shifted to the realm of psychological perception. The enemy knows he can no longer litigate your life from the throne, so he attempts to reconstruct the courtroom within the walls of your own mind. His primary tactic now is the lie of attainment. He whispers that the Father is still auditing your performance, suggesting that the distance between you and the Porch is miles wide and can only be closed by your effort.

This deception creates an inner courtroom where we inadvertently take up the role of the disarmed accuser. We become our own judge, jury, and executioner. We review the footage of our days, analyzing every thought and action through the lens of the old law. Did I pray enough? Was my heart pure enough? Did I really mean it? We sit in the defendant's chair, sweating under the lights of our own scrutiny, unaware that the Judge left the bench long ago to prepare a feast in our honor.

The enemy weaponized fear through the shame of our past failures. By magnifying the weight of our previous mistakes, he attempts to pull us back under the Older Brother's code of legalism. He makes us tremble at the thought of a final verdict, projecting a punitive nature onto the Bēma seat—the judgment seat of Christ—twisting a place of reward into a place of retribution. This anxiety acts like a pair of spiritual noise-canceling headphones; it generates a frequency of fear that doesn't stop the Father from singing His song of love over us, but it effectively prevents us from hearing the melody.

The victory lies in recognizing the hum of that anxiety for what it is: static. The enemy is banking on the hope that if he keeps the noise loud enough, you will never notice the silence of the Law. But we have the power to remove the headphones. We can choose to tune out the lies of attainment and tune into the steady, rhythmic frequency of grace. When we do, we find that the Father hasn't been auditing us; He has been singing over us the whole time.

Shadowboxing the Lie

THE THEOLOGICAL REALITY THAT THE ENEMY IS DISarmed clashes violently with our daily emotional experience.

We know the war is over, but we keep hearing explosions. I spent long seasons intensely shadowboxing, feeling compelled to engage in a fight that was already won. The idea of spiritual warfare captivated me, but I always wondered: How do we actually get anywhere by focusing on a defeated foe?

I found that the moment I shifted my focus away from locking eyes with Jesus; I started detecting evil in everything. Suddenly, every migraine was a principality, every bad mood was a python spirit, and every relational conflict was a demonic assignment. The spiritual theatrics were exhausting. I was putting on the older brother's heavy, ill-fitting armor and running back out to a battlefield that had been silent for two thousand years. I was treating a squatter as if he still owned the house, swinging a sword at creaks in the floorboards.

This is the great deception of the disarmed foe: to get you to mistake the echo of the old battle for the battle itself. He wants you to spend your energy fighting shadows because it keeps you from resting in the substance of Christ. The focus on a defeated enemy is a distraction, a spiritual sleight of hand designed to keep you from enjoying the feast of the Father. You become so busy scanning the horizon for a threat that you miss the celebration happening right in front of you.

Freedom comes not in learning to fight better, but in realizing you don't have to fight at all. It's about laying down the

Older Brother's rusty sword and picking up the Son's fork. It is a conscious choice to shift our gaze from the shadows flitting in our peripheral vision and fix it on the face of Jesus. When we do, the noise of the phantom battle fades, and we hear the music of the party. We stop shadowboxing with lies and start dancing in the living room with One who has already secured our permanent and unassailable peace.

Secured for the Wooing

THE MOMENT I STOPPED FIGHTING THE SYMPTOMS AND instead rested in the Finished Reality of the cross, the shadow dissolved. It did not flee in terror from my spiritual authority; it simply vanished in the presence of a superior reality. The only weapon that neutralizes a lie is the Truth of who you already are—an indivisible child sitting safely on the Father's porch.

Understanding the disarmed enemy is essential to living the Art of Being Wooed. The Father's song of love requires a quiet heart to be heard. You cannot hear a lullaby while you are screaming at a ghost. You cannot feel the warmth of the Porch while you are shivering in a trench of your own making, waiting for an attack that will never come. The battle is not to defeat the darkness but to attune our ears to the ever-present music of light.

Christ's victory secured the Porch for you. He did not just

make it available; He made it your permanent, legal address. He defeated the system of death so completely that the Father's pursuit of your heart is now safe, effective, and un-hindered. You are not pursuing a distant judge, hoping to catch his attention with your good behavior. You are simply responding to the Father who, through Christ, proved His eternal commitment to your secured identity.

The architecture of the shadow is crumbling. It cannot stand in the Porch's light. Every time you choose to tune your ears to the Father's whistle—that low, steady frequency of 'It is finished'—over the frantic, high-pitched alarm of the amygdala, you are tearing down a stone of the old courtroom.

The war is over, even if your body hasn't quite believed the news. You are safe to put down the armor, stop scanning the horizon for a blow, and just breathe the oxygen of the Porch. The shadow has no substance because the Light has already claimed the room.

PART III
THE ONTOLOGICAL SHIFT

Religion is a series of maneuvers; Restoration is a series of realizations.

We have spent lifetimes trying to become what we already are—mastering the maneuvers of performance to earn a seat that was never for sale. But the Landslide has buried the maneuvers. This part of the journey is not about the renovation of your old behaviors, but the realization of your new DNA. You aren't a project to be completed; you are a child of the Father, and you have always belonged to the Dance.

8

The Corresponding Strength

The Ezer and the Parakletos: Reclaiming the Mirror of Identity

IN THE HEBREW, *EZER KENEGDO* IS OFTEN TRANS-
lated as "help-meet," but its literal weight is Corresponding Strength. It is the one who stands face-to-face
(*kenegdo*) to reflect your true nature. An Ezer doesn't provide
what you lack; the Ezer mirrors the abundance you've forgotten you carry. This Finished Work reveals that the "Other
Helper" (*Allon Parakletos*) is not a legal representative sent to
bridge a distance; He is the Cruciform Presence who occupies
the distance until you realize the distance was always a lie. He
doesn't advocate for your acceptance; He advocates *from* your
inclusion.

The Audit of the "Lawyer"

The religious system has a long-standing obsession with
the "Legal Advocate." We have been conditioned to view the
Holy Spirit as a celestial paralegal, a Divine P.I. who spends
His days gathering evidence of our "sincerity" to bolster a defense case we aren't even sure we're winning. In this version of
the story, the Trinity is a house divided. We imagine a Father

who is the primary obstacle to our peace, a Son who is a tireless defense attorney trying to talk a Judge into a plea deal, and a Spirit who acts as the internal auditor, checking our hearts for any sign of unapproved joy.

But the Father is not a Judge who needs to be convinced, and you are not a defendant who needs a lawyer. To understand the Helper, we have to go back before the fall, back before the first "bad" was ever recorded in the audit. In Genesis 2, God looks at the man—whole, unfallen, and perfect—and says something scandalous: "It is not good." Man was not good because he was alone, and in the Kingdom, isolation is the only true poverty. He was a son with no mirror. God didn't give him a servant to manage his chores; He gave him Eve.

Reclaiming the Face of Eve

By naming Eve, we reclaim the original intent of the Witness. Eve was not an afterthought or a secondary citizen; she was the *Ezer*. We must perform a quick surgery on our religious vocabulary here: in the Old Testament, the word *Ezer* is used twenty-one times—sixteen of those times, it refers to God Himself as our help. If *Ezer* is a title God gives Himself, it cannot mean "subordinate assistant." It must mean Indispensable Strength.

Eve was the Strength that corresponded to Adam's own— a face-to-face presence designed for Union. Before the serpent whispered the lie of lack, Eve stood as the biological and spiritual proof of Adam's abundance. She didn't stand behind him to push him; she stood in front of him to show him who he was. In the Kingdom, your identity is not something you find by looking inward at your own navel; it is something that is mirrored back to you by the Face of Love. The Holy Spirit is the "Eve" of our spiritual reality—the one who stands face-to-face with our souls to remind us that we aren't orphans, but heirs.

The Sovereign "No"

I remember a morning that smelled like stale kids' ministry crackers and the heavy, metallic exhaustion of six kids in tow. I was the "Good Angie," the one who kept the files color-coded and the smile pressed. But then the "Management" arrived. The Pastor's wife came with a list of to-do's in a sheer state of control, attempting to flex a title over my being. Typically, the audit in my head would have won. I would have folded, grabbing for the acceptance I thought was my only oxygen.

But that day, the Ezer—that Corresponding Strength—stood face-to-face with my soul. A Strength that didn't belong to my timidity rose in my marrow. This wasn't a "bad Angie" rebellion; it was an "Eve realization." I looked at the list, I looked at the control, and I simply said, "No."

I walked out the door. The sun was still shining, the kids were still sticky, and the world didn't end. But the "Force" had lost its pull. I was still a mother, still a friend, and still a daughter, but I was no longer a project. The aftermath was a clinical study in the courtroom of man. There were phone calls and meetings with Elders where she went into a full-blown melodrama, sobbing in disbelief that I wouldn't cower. She was attempting to use her own sorrow as a gavel to bring me back to the witness stand. But I was bulletproof. The manipulation didn't penetrate because I wasn't defending a case; I was inhabiting a Reality. I wasn't being haughty; I was just heavy with the truth. When they told me I needed to submit to her authority, I realized that if authority is pure of heart, submission is a natural occurrence, not a forced performance.

Wisdom vs. Intellect

I am not an intellectual. I don't sit in the high places of academic posturing. My ontology doesn't come from a syllabus; it comes from a sovereign dependency on a Spirit who has added shocking value to my life.

If you are new to this, you might wonder how a "Spirit" affects your "Cells." It's simple: The Holy Spirit is the Biological Translator of the Father's heart. He doesn't just talk to your "mind"; He addresses your nervous system. When He mirrors your inclusion, the "Redline" of your anxiety drops. He is the oxytocin to the Law's adrenaline.

When I stood in that meeting with those Elders, they were

speaking the language of position and protocol. They had the intellect of the system, but I was tuned into the Wisdom of the Witness. Wisdom isn't knowing the rules of the game; wisdom is realizing that the game is over. The Holy Spirit has bypassed my lack of intellect to give me a surplus of being. In those phone calls, the words that flowed from my lips weren't mine; they were His. I didn't have to prep for a deposition because I wasn't a defendant. I was just a daughter talking to siblings who had forgotten they were children, too.

The Sabbath Rebellion *(The Great Deletion and the Coronation of the Son of Man)*

Revelation isn't a map of a future war; it's an X-ray of what happened on the Cross. We often rush from the "It is finished" of Friday to the "He is risen" of Sunday, treating Holy Saturday like a divine waiting room—a quiet "not yet" between the blood and the glory. But if you look at the architecture of the burial, the Father was performing a symmetric reclamation.

John tells us that in the place where He was crucified, there was a garden, and in the garden, a new tomb (John 19:41). Stop and smell the soil. In Genesis, the first Adam abdicated his dominion in a garden. He traded the "Breath" for the "Dust" and moved into a delusion of lack. On Saturday, the Second Adam—the Son of Man—was laid back into the garden. This wasn't just a burial; it was the Father re-planting the Original Life into the very ground we had surrendered. Saturday wasn't a "day off" for God; it was a Sabbath Rebellion. While the world thought the Hired Hand was in charge of the burial, the Essence was in the basement of humanity, evicting the squatter and incinerating the ledger.

The Miracle of the Mud

We think new creation only arrived when the stone rolled away, but the evidence was already blinking in the eyes of a blind man. When Jesus spit in the dirt to make eyeballs for the man born blind (John 9:6), He was performing a "New Genesis" act. He was proving that creation responds to the Christ-essence. He didn't ask the dirt for permission; He spoke to it as its Source.

This is your Ontological Mandate: You were made from the "Breath" and the "Dust." You don't strive for dominion; you *are* dominion because of the Breath. The only reason we stopped ruling is that we believed the serpent's lie that we weren't already like God. We abdicated. We started trying to "buy" an identity through sacrifice (the way of Cain), forgetting that we were already spoken into existence as "Very Good."

The Mercy Seat X-Ray

If you want to understand what Jesus was actually doing in the belly of the earth, you have to look at the X-ray. In

Daniel 7, we see the "Ancient of Days" take His seat. A river of fire flows out from Him. The court sits, and the books are opened. For centuries, religion has used this image to keep us in the "Audit"—telling us that one day, every secret failure will be read aloud from a cosmic ledger.

But look at the fulfillment in Revelation 20. The books are opened, and then death and Hades are thrown into the lake of fire. Christ is the Lake of Fire. He is the Liquid Love that already consumed the record of your debt. He didn't just pay the bill; He burned the counting house. When the Slain Lamb took the book of our debt, He stepped into the River of Fire flowing from the Father and swallowed death, the grave, and the record of wrongs whole. Love is physically incapable of keeping a record of wrongs (1 Corinthians 13:5), so it simply incinerated the paper. You aren't standing in a docket; you are standing in an ash-heap where your debt used to be.

The Selective Sovereignty of the Hired Hand

We have developed a strange, religious double standard when it comes to the power of God. When a friend receives a terminal diagnosis, when a storm levels a town, or when calamity strikes without warning, the religious system doesn't flinch. We immediately reach for the "Sovereignty Card." We shrug our shoulders and say, "God is sovereign; His ways are not our ways." We have no problem pinning the "Bad" to His character, using His absolute authority as a cosmic rug under which we sweep the things we cannot explain.

But a strange thing happens the moment we move from the calamity to the Cross.

The second we suggest that this same Sovereignty was applied to the Total Reclamation of Humanity—that Jesus actually *finished* the work and brought the "all" into Himself once and for all—everyone suddenly becomes a nuanced theologian. We start looking for the fine print. We begin to argue about what God "can and cannot" accomplish without our permission.

Why is it that we are so comfortable with a God who is in total control of our disasters, but so terrified of a God who is in total control of our Victory?

If we believe God is sovereign enough to allow a "millstone" or a "shingle," why do we doubt He is sovereign enough to apply a Universal Amnesty? This is the "Missing Sovereignty" of the Audit. The religious system loves a Sovereign God who manages consequences, but it fears a Sovereign God who eliminates the Courtroom.

To live on the Porch is to stop being a "theological gatekeeper" for the Father's goodness. If He is Sovereign, then His "It is Finished" was not a proposal submitted for our approval; it was a Royal Decree executed in the flesh. He didn't ask for a vote in the grave, and He didn't wait for your "Amen" to make you New. He simply applied the Life.

We must decide: Is He only sovereign over the "not yet," or is He Sovereign over the "already"? If He is the King of the Finished Work, then the account against you hasn't just been "managed"—it has been Sovereignly Deleted.

The Mission: Discipling the Nations

This is where the "Porch" becomes a "Nations-Shaker." We have busied ourselves thinking we are supposed to go out and "save souls," but Jesus already did that. In His incarnation, He took on the human nature and discipled it back into Union. He lived the perfect life *as* us, then died and rose *as* us. He brought the "all" into Himself. Your job isn't to save people; it's to awaken them to the reality that is already theirs.

The Great Commission isn't about making disciples of people—Jesus already reclaimed the human species in His own body. The Commission is to go and make disciples of the nations (Matthew 28:19). Creation is groaning for the sons and daughters of glory to take their rightful place (Romans 8). When you walk into a room as an image-bearer who knows the trial is over, the "Mud" starts to blink. You aren't a spiritual salesman; you are a Sovereign Presence. You walk near someone, and because you are a new creation teeming with life, they awaken to their own unfolding in Christ. Jesus did His job in the flesh. Now, let's do ours.

The Trinitarian Circuit: A Oneness Anatomy

The mystery of our security isn't found in a legal plea, but in a biological Union. To understand the Union Jesus prayed for, we have to move away from the idea of a "line" and toward the reality of a Current. You aren't a spectator watching this; you are inhabiting it. We keep the Greek terms here— *Thelēma, Enōsis, Parakletos*—not as barriers, but as anchors for our Home.

The Father is the *Thelēma*—the Will. Think of Him as the Architect who dreamed up the house and left the porch light on. He is the origin of the feast who is already convinced of your value, and His Will isn't a list of requirements; it is His settled purpose. He is the eternal "Yes" toward your life. Beside Him, the Son stands as the *Enōsis*—the Solidarity. He is the point where the Divine and the Human were fused forever, the "Front Door" where God and Man happen to occupy the same space. He doesn't advocate for your acceptance; He advocates *from* your inclusion.

And then there is the Spirit, the *Parakletos* acting as our Ezer, the Mirror. He is the one who walks you to the hallway mirror of the house to show you that you're already wearing the family signet ring. He doesn't bring new information; He takes the finished fact of that Union and reflects it to your heart, mirroring the abundance of the Christ-life you already carry.

Just as Eve stood face-to-face with Adam to reflect his nature, the Spirit stands face-to-face with your soul. Because of this *Koinōnia*—the Participation—this circuit isn't just something we observe; it's something we inhabit. Our existence isn't a waiting room for an escape; it is a throne room for an occupation. We are the "Yes" of God made visible. We aren't trying to leave; we are learning to occupy this reality as kings and priests. The Spirit is the Mirror reflecting the Solidarity of the Son to fulfill the perfect Will of the Father on earth as it is in heaven.

The Geography of Forgetting

This circuit is built on a finished geography. Scripture tells us that God has removed our transgressions as far as the east is from the west (Psalm 103:12) and thrown our sins into the sea of forgetfulness (Micah 7:19). This isn't just a poetic way to say we're "off the hook." It means the Father has intentionally placed our "mess-ups" in a location He no longer visits. He isn't going to go deep-sea diving to recover the very things the Son's death already dissolved. He isn't going to rail against His own death by bringing up the file He's already burned.

The cosmic courtroom is just a stage built by the hired hand to manage control. The *Parakletos* doesn't defend you from God; He defends you *with* God. He is the seal of a finished reality, the one who makes you bulletproof to the melodrama because He has already shown you that the Father isn't weighing you—He is wearing you. I've stopped waiting for a verdict because the door has been standing open all along. I've stopped believing in a begging Jesus because I've met a Dancing King who is already sharing His seat with me.

9

The Nicodemus Trap And The Resonance Of The Lamb

T HE AIR IN THE SANCTUARY WAS THICK, BUT IT wasn't the weight of the Glory; it was the stagnant, pressurized humidity of a "Good Christian" recruitment drive. I sat in the crowd as the guest speaker paced the stage, wielding a slideshow of orphans like a collection of legal briefs. The subtext wasn't a celebration of life; it was an audit of our sincerity. The pitch was a clinical maneuver: *If you were truly a follower of Christ, your home would be open. If you were a "Good Christian," you would bridge this gap.*

It was a "do-gooder" ploy that turned a sovereign movement of the heart into a high-stakes audition for moral standing. But as the guilt rose in the room, I felt that familiar, localized "burn" in my own chest—the one I had carried for years as a Children's Pastor. It was the physical protest of a tribal instinct that knew, deep down, that religious ideation is a dangerously fragile bridge to build over the complexities of a human heart.

The Tribal Wall and the DNA Ease

I'll be the first to admit that I've sat in that crowd carrying my own version of tribal arrogance. Back when my own six children were young and the days were a blur of constant demand, I lived under the assumption that because my heart was full, my capacity was infinite. Many thought my "mother-heart" was a bridge strong enough to carry any load.

They were wrong.

In the middle of my own exhaustion, I discovered a hard, jagged border within my own biology: I had little tolerance for "noise" that wasn't of my own flesh. There is a reality that many families with both biological and adoptive children are terrified to face: the "DNA Ease." With your own flesh and blood, there is a subconscious rhythm, a shared frequency that requires no translation. You understand their cries, you anticipate their moods, and your nervous system "tunes" into theirs with a natural fluidity.

But when a child enters the home who doesn't share that DNA echo—bringing a different temperamental "static" or the jagged edge of trauma—the ease vanishes. In the Adam-flesh, this "otherness" triggers a Sympathetic spike. Your heart rate climbs, your chest tightens, and the child's presence becomes a biological friction. We are biologically wired for Limbic Resonance—the subconscious way our nervous systems "tune" into the internal states of those we recognize as our own. When that resonance is absent, the nervous system sees "threat" where the Sunday School lesson says "neighbor." This is the Vagus nerve in reverse; instead of calming you, the "otherness" triggers an alarm.

The Innocence of Ignorance

I HAVE READ THE DEVASTATING NEWS ARTICLES OF PARents who find themselves locking a child in a room, reacting with a coldness that borders on neglect, or simply drowning in a silent, mutual resentment. I have seen the "cringe" of an adoptive father who hears the word "Daddy" from a child whose DNA isn't resonant with his own—a sound that, instead of bringing joy, triggers an internal biological alarm.

We want to call these parents monsters, but I see the innocence of ignorance. They are responding from a nervous system that hasn't learned the language of a "New Source." They are trying to run a "Merged Family" on a "Tribal Operating System," and they are being shredded by the friction. They are trying to solve a Union-deficit with religious effort.

The child is caught in the same loop. I have looked into the eyes of adopted children whose only language is the Narrative of Rejection. Because their biology is wired for the "Other," they will subconsciously force everyone into scenarios that *require* them to be rejected. They will agitate and sabotage until you confirm their deepest, Adam-flesh fear: *I do not belong here.* This analysis isn't a rant; it is a diagnostic. Until we address the reality of Oneness, we will always attempt to legislate the symptoms of a sleeping humanity.

The Mirror of the "Other"

WE MUST SEE THAT THE FRICTION IN THE ADOPTIVE home is not an isolated crisis; it is a localized X-ray of the global tribal heart. We reject each other for the exact same reasons that adoption proves difficult outside of Union. In the Adam-delusion, we are convinced that our safety lies in our Separation.

If a child doesn't share my DNA, my system flags them as a 'stranger.' If a neighbor doesn't share my doctrine, my system flags them as an 'enemy.' If a nation doesn't share my borders, my system flags them as a 'threat.' This is the high cost of tribalism: a life spent defending a fortress of 'Self' against a world of 'Other.'

The Spirit of Adoption as the Global Cure

THIS IS WHY THE SPIRIT OF ADOPTION IS THE ONLY FUNCtional answer for the nations. It isn't a warm sentiment; it is the ontological collapse of 'Otherness.' When we awaken to Union, we realize that the 'noise' we were trying to reject in the child—or the neighbor, or the nation—is actually the sound of our own Life-Source in a different frequency.

We stop trying to 'tolerate' the stranger and begin to recognize the sibling. The 'Abba' cry is the sound of the tribal wall falling down, proving that when we are 'cut into' the Son, the hardware of rejection is replaced by the resonance of the Lamb.

The Nicodemus Trap: The Womb of Effort

THIS BIOLOGICAL FRICTION CREATES THE NICODEMUS Trap. Nicodemus was the elite of the elite, a PhD in the machinery of the flesh. But he came to Jesus by night because he had reached the end of what that hardware could produce. He wasn't looking for a new rule; he was looking for a new Origin.

We fall into the same trap when we attempt to fix the "cringe" or the "burn" by crawling back into a womb of "trying harder." We ask, *"How can I be more inclusive?"* while the Father is standing on the Porch asking, *"Do you know who you are?"* Whether the crisis is the orphan, the unborn, or the incarcerated, these issues remain unsolvable outside of Union. We treat the act of abortion or the act of crime as the root, but the root is the thought of separation—the belief that we are separate from our Source and therefore separate from our Brother. As Ephesians 2:14 declares, Christ has broken down the middle wall of partition between us.

The Trail of Evidence: The Co-Incision

To understand how we move past the tribal wall, we have to look at the Trail of Evidence left by the Father. The victory wasn't a reaction to our failure; it was the pre-temporal blueprint. Revelation 13:8 tells us Christ is the *"Lamb slain from the foundation of the world."* The "Co-Incision" was the plan before the first breath was taken.

When Christ's flesh was torn, He wasn't just a man bleeding; He was the Last Adam gathering the entire human genome into His own body. In Colossians 2:11-12, we see this "circumcision made without hands." This was the species-level Co-Incision. Every tribe, tongue, and nation was legally and ontologically "cut into" His death so they could be "exhaled" into His life. You aren't recruiting strangers to a cause; you are announcing a shared DNA to a family that has forgotten its name.

Under the Influence: The Resurrection Coup

The answer to tribalism isn't a better agency; it is the Incarnation. When Christ took on flesh, He hijacked the human genome and re-coded the frequency of what it means to be human. On Good Friday, the "It is Finished" was a biometrical signature. Christ dissolved the walls of the counting house and gathered every fragmented frequency into His own body.

In this new reality, our ability to cry "Abba, Father" is not a religious duty; it is a visceral reflex dependent on our awakening to Union. The Spirit of Adoption is the ontological realization that there is no stranger. You cannot truly cry "Abba" for a child who is "other"—and that child cannot find their "Abba"—until you realize you are sharing the exact same Life-Source. We move from "taking someone in" to recognizing a sibling who was always meant for the Porch.

The Paschal Exhale: Every Tribe, Every Tongue

THIS IS THE "WOW" OF THE NEW CREATION: WE ARE raised to life under the total, saturating influence of Resurrection Power.

I see a vision of Jesus walking out of that tomb, and as He steps into the morning air, He releases a single, cosmic Exhale. From that breath emerges a people who are colorful, vibrant, and possessed by the knowledge of His image. They aren't standing around the graveyard clinging to His feet; they land and they run. Within that Resurrection on Paschal Sunday, the era of striving, earning, and sacrificing was incinerated. In its place, He installed Dunamis Life.

This is the "5th Gospel" reality: If Revelation is our map,

then the bowing of the knee isn't a future threat—it is a current, underlying reality of the New Creation. What if we've been waiting for a day that has already occurred in the Spirit? What if, in the split-second of the Co-Incision, the knees of every tribe and tongue didn't just bend out of duty, but buckled under the weight of a Love they finally recognized as their own Source? Our tongues are already confessing to the nations that Jesus Christ is Lord, because the victory is objective and the species has been reclaimed.

Priests and Kings: Legislating Love

As Priests and Kings, we don't "try" to love; we legislate Love. We are an ambassadorial people. We no longer fight over semantically charged labels—that is an underdog approach. We stand as Resurrection Life and refuse to allow verbiage to be an irritant.

We aren't legislating form, morality, or semantics; we are legislating a life-altering Union. We see the King standing with the keys of death and Hades firmly in His hands. But the mystery is this: While the keys remain in His hands, the dominion over creation has been placed in ours.

The audit is over. The tribal walls have been incinerated by Liquid Love. Now, release the resounding cry of Abba and go make disciples of the nations. The 12 tribes are home, the hardware of rejection has been deleted, and the earth is waiting for the frequency of the Sons.

10

Rebirth Of The Indivisible

Ontology: Your fundamental nature. In the Kingdom, your original design is New Creation. It isn't a behavior you manage; it's your DNA.

The Genetic Miracle of Grace

We have spoken of the eviction of the squatter; now let us look into the renovation of the house. It is one thing to know that the enemy is disarmed; it is another thing entirely to realize that your very nature has been rewritten. The Cross, as the kiss of justice, was not merely a moment of theological reconciliation; it was the most significant moment of new creation since the Garden of Eden. Most of us learned a teflon version of salvation—where God's grace merely coats a fundamentally dirty person. We are told we are, "sinners saved by grace," a phrase that suggests we are still broken creatures a divine tarp merely covers. But the Father on the Porch is not interested in tarps; He is interested in the very substance—the nature of your being.

The Final Act: Blood and Water

THE CLIMAX OF THE CRUCIFIXION WAS NOT THE DEATH itself, but the public, visible proof of what that death accomplished. The Apostle John recounts that when the Roman soldier pierced Christ's side, immediately there came out blood and water (John 19:34). This flow is the definitive statement that Amnesty and our new nature are inseparable. The Blood signifies the final atonement, satisfying the broken system's demands—the perpetrator paid in full the legal penalty for the Lie of Attainment. The Water signifies the Holy Spirit and the new, spiritual life—the life-giving current of the river. Together, they announce that the Father's ultimate act of justice was the rebirth of His children.

The Anatomy of a Shell

I SPENT YEARS FEELING LIKE MY IDENTITY WAS A HOUSE of cards. As a child, I did not just lack confidence; I lacked a sense of permission to exist. My mother's legs were my primary fortress, and I perpetually anchored myself behind them against a world that felt too loud and too inquisitive. When I wasn't hiding behind her, I was finding pockets of solitude where I could play unseen, tucked away in the shadows where the Audit of social expectation couldn't find me.

This timidity was not a choice; it was geography. Living only seconds away from my elementary school provided a dangerous relief. When the pressure of being perceived by teachers or peers became too heavy, I would simply vanish. I would walk off the school grounds and retreat to the only place that felt safe: home. It was a quick fix for a soul that felt constantly measured. But there was a tragic irony in my escape. I was fleeing the Judgment of the classroom for a house that was its own kind of minefield. Drugs were hidden in this same home, and I would eventually sit there as a DARE student while my home life mocked the curriculum. Yet, to my young, nervous system, the known chaos of that house was still preferable to the public exposure of the schoolyard. I was choosing the shadow I knew over the scales I couldn't balance. I was retreating to a porch that was crumbling, simply because it was the only porch I had.

As I grew, the shell only hardened. Straight, focused attention felt like a heat lamp on wax. Laughter and joking were not invitations to joy; they were paralyzing puzzles I couldn't solve. I couldn't order a pizza over the phone, have a one-on-one conversation without a racing heart, or even ask for the paycheck I had rightfully earned. If people were looking at me, I assumed they didn't like me. I inhabited the identity of a defendant, even if I was doing everything right, because I was constantly looking for a space to hide.

The Lens of Amnesty (Legal)	The Lens of Ontology (Nature)
Status: A pardoned criminal.	Identity: A beloved child.
Location: The Courtroom.	Location: The Porch.
Focus: Cleaning the record.	Focus: Realizing the design.
Goal: To become "good enough."	Goal: To rest in "Finished."
Effort: Managing the fruit.	Source: Abiding in the Root.

The Surge in the Sanctuary

BUT AS I ENTERED ADULTHOOD, AN UNQUENCHABLE HUN-ger for God consumed me. I would pepper seasoned Christians with deep, gnawing questions, only to find they were profoundly uncomfortable with hunger. They wanted me to stay in the lines; I wanted to touch the fire. This hunger led to a Sunday morning when I had signed up to be water baptized. But God didn't wait for the lake. I had been trembling all morning—a physical shaking I couldn't control. I hadn't even made it out of the church building when a power I had never felt before flushed me out. A wave of what had me quivering washed over me. Right there, before the ritual could begin, the King claimed His territory.

We eventually left the building to go to the lake for a cookout followed by the baptisms. I can honestly say I do not remember the ceremony at all. An encounter, an experience that carved out a greater depth in me and changed who I was forever, baptized me. As I sat on the edge of the lake, perched upon a large boulder that doubled as my mercy seat, the world had become unrecognizable. The green of the grass and the leaves on the trees were no longer one-dimensional; they had layers, beckoning me to look deeper. The blue sky was suddenly a masterpiece composed of a thousand shades of blue. I wondered if my eyes had opened for the first time—if I had awakened from a lifelong dream or discovered I had been colorblind my entire life. The difference was visceral: my skin felt the wind and my eyes drank in the deep blue of the sky.

The Adam and Eve Parallel

TO TRULY APPRECIATE THIS , WE MUST ANCHOR IT IN THE original design. Just as the first woman, Eve, was brought forth from the side of a sleeping Adam, the New Creation—the Church—was brought forth from the side of the wounded second Adam, Christ. The First Adam slept, allowing life to be physically birthed from his rib. The Second Adam's death allowed His side to physically birth spiritual, eternal life. This parallelism shows that your new identity is not an afterthought. You are the continuation of humanity's original design, restored and made incorruptible. This identity is inherently Indivisible, created from the essence of the wounded, resurrected King.

We must realize that our standing was never a legal reprieve, or a stayed sentence. We didn't just receive a pardon that left our old selves intact; we were brought forth into a new origin. Out of the blood and water of the Crucified Christ, a nature was born that cannot be un-made, and a standing was established that cannot be revoked. Our verdict wasn't written on a scroll to be filed away in a courtroom; it was woven into the very fabric of our being. We weren't just given a second chance at an old life; we were swallowed by the life of the Son.

The Architecture of the Millstone

JUSTICE, WHEN VIEWED THROUGH THE TRANSACTIONAL ledger of retribution, is a hungry thing. It demands a pound of flesh to balance the record of pain. I had fed those accounts with my own deep sadness. In the logic of the world—and even in the logic of the religious systems I had been raised in— his destruction would have been my peace. I felt I had every right to demand payment for the violation of our home and the stolen innocence of our daughters. But the river of Reconciliation does not flow toward destruction; it flows toward the restoration of all things.

I remember a day when the weight of that wreckage finally broke me. I wasn't sitting in a quiet prayer closet; I was in a dark alleyway of sadness and terror. I left the house abruptly, got into our family Suburban, and drove aimlessly. My vision was so blurred by tears that the road ahead was a smear of gray. I was trying to outrun a pain that seemed to have no exit. In my despair, a rogue thought flew toward me with terrifying clarity: *At the next intersection, send a car to take me out.* It wasn't just a thought; it was a petition.

Terrified by the depth of the darkness, I pulled over on a lonely country road and wailed. I don't even know if words came out, but I know He heard my tears. In the middle of that wail, the Father's response came—not as a lecture, but as a key: "Angie, can what I've done count toward him now?"

The question didn't need an explanation. I knew exactly what He was asking. I had been questioning how this monster could be included in what Jesus had accomplished on the cross. I knew my heart was stuck, but I couldn't find a way out. That question was the click of the lock. I wailed in agreement, realizing it was never in my hands to begin with, and understood that my own freedom depended on me agreeing with God's goodness—even for the inexcusable.

Then, He pulled back the veil. I wasn't looking at a monster who was getting away with a crime; I was looking at a prisoner. In a vision, I saw him standing there, bound by massive, rusted chains that were anchored to millstones at his feet. He wasn't flourishing; he was living in a perpetual state of drowning, suffocated by the very weight of the life he had chosen. The Father whispered, 'It is not my character to tie the millstone. But this is the architecture of the life he has chosen.'

The Dancing Conquest

With a heart that finally stopped demanding payment, I stepped toward him in that vision. I reached out and began to unwrap the weighty chains from around his body. One by one, I let the millstones drop into the depths. I wasn't just freeing him; I was freeing myself from the labor of being his jailer.

As the last millstone sank, the scene shifted with a jarring, cinematic speed. The dark alleyway of my trauma evaporated, and I was suddenly standing in the middle of a massive, multitribe assembly. The atmosphere was electric, and in the center of it all was a boxing ring.

I was still in the middle of a wail, my vision blurred and

tears still streaming down my face from the weight of the forgiveness I had just touched. I was trying to keep up with the movement of the Spirit, still breathless from the click of the lock, when I looked into the ring. I did not observe a fight. I didn't see a blow. I saw a Man.

He was in the center of that ring, dancing. And He wasn't just doing a polite religious two-step. Aside from the theology of it all, the theatrics were comically glorious to reconsider—disco lights and bell bottoms, friends! But the way He danced wasn't typical; He never slowed down. It was a dance that seemed to go on and on, fueled by an unbridled, funky joy that mocked the very gravity of the courtroom I had just left.

Jesus, the Dancing Man.

My heart soars and my eyes well up at the mere thought of it: He was dancing on injustice. This dance wasn't just for my benefit; it was for the cousin as well. The Dancer was conquering the very injustice that had led that man's mind to reach toward the life of a predator. He wasn't just ignoring the mess; He was out-dancing the darkness, reclaiming the original design of the violated and the violator alike.

The juxtaposition was uncanny. How could the unwrapping of chains lead directly to a disco in a boxing ring? At that moment, I was touching the *Perichoresis*—the eternal, joyful

Divine Dance of the Trinity. The profound grace the Father carried me through that day broke open my understanding of the dance. A dancer who had already won had hijacked the boxing ring—the place where the world expects us to fight for our fairness or defend our wounds. I realized that the Father doesn't just want us pardoned; He wants us in the rhythm of a victory that never stops.

If you feel a sense of holy whiplash moving from the dark alleyway of those millstones to a boxing ring filled with disco lights, believe me—I felt it too. It is a jarring, almost offensive transition to the logical mind. We want the resolution of our trauma to be a somber, quiet affair—a clinical closing of a file. But the Father's restoration isn't a library; it's a celebration. He doesn't just want to 'process' our pain; He wants to out-dance it. This shift from the wail to the ditty isn't a dismissal of the wreckage; it's a sovereign declaration that the wreckage no longer has the floor. The Dancer has taken the lead.

The Secure, Finished Identity

LIVING AS AN INDIVISIBLE CHILD CHANGES THE WAY WE handle our wounds. That miracle on the country road didn't happen because I finally worked through my issues; it happened because I finally agreed with a reality that had been true all along. The apostle Paul makes this declaration the cornerstone of the reconciled life: *Therefore, if anyone is in Christ, he is a new creation. The old has passed away; behold, the new has come* (2 Corinthians 5:17).

Your identity is complete, finished, and whole. The question is no longer, *Am I enough yet?* I already am, that's the answer. The only choice left is to live from this reality, even when the reality of your circumstances is screaming.

During the hardest of seasons, as I walked through the fire with my daughters, the enemy wanted me to believe that my pain was proof of my separation. But because I am indivisible from Him, He was suffering with me. He wasn't a distant observer; He was the Emmanuel standing in the terrors of those days. In those first months, I was raw—unhinged and hurting. My thoughts were nonsensical; my body was failing under the weight of the stress—shingles covered my back and my eyelids were thick with eczema. I spent my days in the darkness of my bedroom, inconsolable. Yet, no matter where my imagination led me in that darkness, I was constantly aware of a Presence.

I had an ongoing daydream that felt more real than the room I was in: I was in a hospital bed, hooked up to machines tracking my vitals. I would drift in and out of consciousness, wildly groggy, as if I were living in a thick fog. But there was a man who sat next to my bedside; he never once left. Every time

I would wake, he would reach out, touch my arm, and simply say, "Stay with me."

His words were so full of weight. I knew he wasn't asking me to get better or wake up; he asked that wherever I was going—into the fog, into the pain, or into the darkness—I find Him there. To acknowledge that even in the hospital bed of my soul, we were still indivisible. He provided the guarantee that I was already found, even when I couldn't find myself.

The Hypostatic Guarantee

To fully grasp the security of this rebirth—the rebirth that allows a mother to unwrap the chains of a predator—we must understand the Hypostatic Union: the doctrine that Christ is fully God and fully Man, united in one single person forever. Christ did not temporarily visit humanity; He permanently united the Divine with the human.

Imagine trying to make an object fireproof. You can spray it with a chemical coating (Amnesty), which works until the coating wears off. Or, you can change the material itself—replacing flammable wood with non-combustible steel. Your unity is based on Christ's Being, not your performance. You are indivisibly one. Christ permanently united the Divine with the human nature; He didn't just save individuals, He salvaged the species. You are included in the Divine Dance not because you stepped onto the floor, but because the Lead Dancer has already picked you up.

The Mandate and the Mountain

ONCE YOU REALIZE SOMEONE HAS PICKED YOU UP, YOU can no longer stay quiet. For a long season, this message of love and identity percolated inside me. I was desperate to speak it, but that old shadow of childhood timidity would occasionally try to hedge me back in.

I remember a specific day at the grocery store during the Christmas season. A Salvation Army ringer was at the door, her voice dancing through the aisles. As I walked toward the exit, she immediately changed course, belting out, "Go tell it on the mountain that Jesus Christ is born!" Those lyrics broke through the last walls of my old shell. It was a mandate moment. I knew without a doubt that I was a Bringer of Truth. The identity of marksman and mastermind that the Lord had spoken over me in a former season wasn't a reward for good behavior; it was a description of my nature.

Trading Religious Jargon for the Vocabulary of the Son

ONCE THE MANDATE IS ACCEPTED, THE DICTIONARY HAS to change. You cannot tell the Truth of the Son using the vocabulary of the Slave. If you spend enough time in a foreign country, you eventually stop translating in your head. You think in the native tongue. The tragedy for many of us is that the plantation still colonizes our speech, even though our nature has been restored. We sit on the porch, yet we still use the vocabulary of the courtroom. We are still speaking the language of debt, retribution, and attainment. I know how exhausting it is to translate your freedom constantly into a language that keeps the religious managers comfortable. But at some point, the native tongue of the Son must become our only dialect.

The Adjective Leash

I HAVE DEVELOPED A PHYSICAL ITCH WHEN I HEAR PEOPLE attempt to qualify their humanity with religious adjectives. In the circles I once ran in, we didn't just have men and women; we had Strong Biblical Men and Powerful Biblical Women. At first glance, these sound like affirmations. But they are actually performance grades. Labeling someone a 'Strong Biblical Man' publicly declares his successful management of specific criteria. It's an audit of his compliance, not a description of his being. It is the good mask on a global scale—a desperate attempt to front a religious reputation so we don't have to face the terrifying possibility of being unmanaged.

We use these labels as spiritual currency. We puff our

chests and lean into these titles to prove we belong in the inner circle. But I want to invite you to look past the titles to the heart of the Father: He isn't looking for a Biblical Man; He is looking for a son. He isn't looking for a Powerful Woman; He is looking for His daughter. The adjectives we use to build ourselves up are the very things that keep us at a distance from the unadorned gaze of the Father. They are the clothing we use to hide our nakedness—the fig leaves of the modern plantation.

We peacock with these titles because we are still trying to prove we deserved the Barabbas exchange. We are still standing on the platform, terrified that if we don't earn our release, someone will realize the wrong person walked free. But the Father doesn't want an employee who has mastered the manual; He wants the child who knows they got a deal they didn't deserve and has stopped trying to pay it back.

I remember a time before the cautionary tales set in—a season where laughter was so thick it felt like a physical substance. I was playing with 'Dad's' tools in the shed, not understanding the power I was handling, yet using them with a thin filter and a wide-open heart. I'd look at a menu and ask Jesus what He'd enjoy eating, because the Oneness wasn't a doctrine; it was a dinner date. It culminated in a ridiculous, lovesick ditty that poured out of me: 'Going to the malt shop, locking eyes with Jesus.' We even turned it into a head-banging screamo rendition. It was wild. Joy was felt. It was the sound of someone who had finally forgotten they were supposed to be managed. It was the native tongue of the Porch—a language where the only adjective that matters is mine.

But the tragedy of the Audit is that it cannot leave a dinner date alone. It sees the unmanaged joy of the Porch and immediately looks for a way to put it to work.

The Architecture of the Asset vs. The Asset and the Manager

I understand the weight of these labels because I entered the center of that system with a clear view of my purpose. Speaking my mind was natural, and I never felt the need to audition. I walked in aware that the gifts at my disposal were assets—tools designed to build, bridge, and see a dream meld into fruition. I worked tirelessly, fueled by a heart that was admittedly half duty and half heart. The truth about my nature is that I don't mind the work; I gain a deep, ontological satisfaction from the labor of bringing a vision to life.

But even when you have the correct perspective of your purpose, you can still feel the friction within the mechanics. This is the tragic limitation of the Hired Hand nature: it cannot distinguish between an investment and a tool's utility. To a manager of a plantation, a tireless heart isn't a peer to be celebrated, but a momentum to be managed. In that environment, the very satisfaction you find in 'doing your part' is eventually audited for how well it supports the existing script. If your momentum outpaces the Manager's comfort, you are no longer being nurtured; you are being used as a scaffold for someone else's limelight.

The Gaps in the Scaffolding

THE CLOSER I GOT TO THE INNER WORKINGS OF THAT ENvironment, the more the structural gaps became visible. My natural inclination is to build, and building often requires identifying what is broken. I saw the decline, and I knew I had the tools to bridge the fractures. I spoke from a place of awareness, not seeking permission but offering a solution to lighten the load. But in a jurisdiction governed by the Hired Hand, a builder with an unscripted voice is perceived as a threat.

The dialect of the plantation cannot handle a peer-to-peer conversation because its entire architecture is built on the preservation of a hierarchy. Instead of the authentic vulnerability that sonship allows—where a simple confession of insecurity could have cleared the air—the system defaulted to its age-old survival theatrics. Gossip, slander, and backstabbing are merely the mechanical smoke of a nature that is terrified of any dream it didn't author.

I then realized that my tireless work only received a welcome when it served as silent support for the status quo. The moment the Daughter of Vision spoke the truth of the gaps she saw, the structural frequency changed. It wasn't a personal rejection of my performance; it was a system failure of a nature that had forgotten how to live on the Porch.

The Cost of the Unscripted Voice

SCARCITY FORMS THE LANGUAGE OF THE RELIGIOUS SYSTEM. It assumes that the river is actually a series of gated puddles that must be managed. You can hear it in the way we talk about our faith: I'm just trying to be faithful, or I'm pressing in for a fresh impartation. This language suggests that God is a distant landlord who rewards the most eloquent, or the most exhausted. It is the language of the far country. The moment I stopped acting as a versatile asset and began to speak from my own internal conviction, the dialect turned on me. The Daughter of Vision became unsubmissive in their eyes. They called the indispensable ingredient deceived.

This is the mechanical cruelty of the religious system: adjectives are used to manage your behavior. The religious system's mechanical cruelty manages your behavior with adjectives. They dangle the idea of being an important player to keep you building their structure, but when you speak with the raw voice of a daughter, they strip your titles to punish you. Words become weapons to isolate anyone who doesn't fit the script.

Being Without Apology

THE MOST RADICAL THING YOU CAN DO IS SPEAK THE truth of your identity without a religious qualifier. It feels exposed at first. It feels like you are walking around naked without your titles or your 'The Lord told me' defenses. But that nakedness is the goal. Christ stripped the enemy so we could stop hiding behind the labels. We move from achieving to abiding. We stop fronting and start existing. When you refuse to use the peacocking language of the religious camp—when you stop trying to validate your existence through spiritual jargon—you are finally letting your true nature show.

The truth is often too quiet for a system built on noise: You are no longer a project to be managed; you are a child who is already home. Rather than grading your goodness, the Father is enjoying your wholeness. Anything more than this is usually just the old Hired Hand in our heads trying to justify a gift that was always free. We are learning to speak a language where finished isn't just a theological term—it's the only breath we need to draw.

11

The Freedom Of The Tributary

The Architecture of the Echo

THE IDENTITY OF 'MARKSMAN' AND 'MASTERMIND' wasn't a reward for good behavior; it was a description of my nature. But once you realize you are a Bringer of Truth, you quickly realize that the world—and the religious systems within it are filled with those who profit from the shadows.

How does a son become a Hired Hand? We imagine it's a cold, calculated decision to seek power—but in my experience, it's a 'falling into." It is an accidental slide into a survival posture. We don't wake up and decide to be a mercenary; we simply wake up and realize we no longer believe the Father is enough.

We pick up the badge of the Hired Hand to cover an old, nagging narrative of lack. We attempt to use the utility of our service to hide the ache of our soul. Sadly, this often reflects the way others treated us. We fall into the same entrapment that once hurt us, believing that if we can just enforce the rules well enough, we can finally protect ourselves from the very sting we are now inflicting on others.

The Two Voices of John 10

THIS NATURE, AS DEFINED BY JESUS, HELPS US IDENTIFY why we feel so revolting when trapped in the badge's survival. He says the Hired Hand runs because he is a Hired Hand and cares nothing for the sheep. This isn't about a lack of human kindness, but a lack of foundational belonging. A Hired Hand is an employee of a brand; he has a contract, not a covenant. The system's reputation and the limelight fundamentally tether him. Therefore, when the wolf enters the room—the wolf of a brother's scandal, the wolf of a family's messy wreckage, or the wolf of a truth that doesn't fit the script—the Hired Hand must run. He has to protect his own good label to survive the audit. He cannot afford the mess of a wounded sheep because he is still trying to prove he belongs at the table by keeping the table clean.

The Sterile Trap: The Seduction of Attainment

EARLY ON IN MY MINISTRY LIFE, I FELL INTO THIS VERY trap. I was desperately trying to attain enough biblical knowledge to fit in, convinced that my proximity to the porch was measured by the precision of my theology. I was a daughter who had fallen into the lie of attainment.

I carried myself in a manner that wasn't inviting, but revolting—a sterile, guarded version of a person who was busy trying to prove she was enough by knowing enough. I was trading the story for the statistics. I was so busy managing the details about Him I lost the delight in Him. I was a Hired Hand of the letter, forgetting that the Spirit is the only thing that breathes life.

The Sovereign Inquisition: The Lifting of the Chin

During that sterile season, God interrupted my frantic becoming. He didn't use a theological debate; He used a question that hit the bullseye of my intention, "What are you doing?"

He has an uncanny way of stripping away the badge with a single inquiry. As if He gently lifted my chin to find myself in Him, He spoke the words that still vibrate in my marrow, "Angie, I have never talked to or taught you in the same manner that you are approaching details about me. I have shared my life with you in a story, in delight, tears, and laughter."

He was inviting me back to the shepherd's frequency. A shepherd doesn't lead through sterile audits; He leads through shared life. He was asking me to stop being a manager of His reputation and my own, and start being a daughter who simply flows in the same way He captured my heart in the first place: story, shared life, and love.

The End of the Scorecard: Shared Life

When the Father spoke about story, delight,

tears, and laughter, He wasn't giving me a new communication style; He was giving me a new ontological rhythm. He revealed that the tributary doesn't carry a clipboard.

The church has, in many corners, forgotten who she is. She has behaved like a middle-manager, perpetually grappling for position and posturing for prominence, as if the Father's love were a limited resource that must be guarded by the most qualified among us. We have spent our energy fighting a defeated enemy and auditing the worthiness of our brothers, never realizing that Love—the very river we claim to represent—does not keep a record of wrong.

If the river doesn't keep a record, how can we? When we truly immerse ourselves in the Father, we lose the ability to keep score. We become unprofitable to the system of audit because we are no longer interested in the currency of debt. We possess a reckless, unmanaged abandon as we sit and love.

The Social Blackout: The Mercy of the Cold Room

I know the cold reality of the social blackout. It is a peculiar nightmare that begins with a subtle shift in the wind—written words that lose their warmth, moving from the shared language of a common vision to the clinical, jagged tone of an indictment. I spent weeks trying to talk over that growing silence, white-knuckling a positive perspective and believing the best, while the frequency of the relationship was already changing.

We eventually found ourselves under the same roof as the Audit, in a collision with a system that had already decided our hearts were second-class. In that environment, the atmosphere didn't just turn cold; it became a vacuum. I realized with sickening clarity that my very heartbeat was unapproved. No matter the effort, no matter the bridge I attempted to build, the disparaging verdict of my origin met me. I was too "American," too "unmanaged," too much of a "person" and not enough of a "product." I have never endured such poor treatment, nor have I felt such a sharp jealousy that it felt like a physical blade.

It felt like a physical drop in temperature. My chest would tighten and my hands would go cold, as if the radiator of the relationship had been shut off by a master switch. This is the mechanical cruelty of the system: your warmth is a wage. As long as you are the workhorse—producing the utility the system demands while staying out of the way of its limelight—the lights stay on. But the moment you drop the badge and stop providing the utility, the circuit breaks. The room grows cold not because the people in it are monsters, but because the system they are serving has no vocabulary for a child who just wants to be.

I realize now that this shift wasn't personal; it was mechanical. Like Dorothy in Oz, I was being haunted by a delusion of distance. The slinging of accusations and the noise of a group mind that wants to edit your heartbeat are just Technicolor special effects designed to keep you serving a Wizard who has no actual power over your nature. Looking back from the Porch, I can see that the social blackout was actually my sovereign impasse. The system didn't reject me; it simply ran out of the currency I was no longer willing to use.

If you are currently standing in that cold room, do not mistake the silence of the system for the silence of the Father. The Father isn't in the bubble with the Wizard; He's on the ground, in the mud, with the daughter who was brave enough to let the Audit fail her. Being ejected from the courtroom will show you that you've always belonged on a porch. You don't have to defend your heartbeat to a machine; you simply have to wake up and realize the dream of separation is over. You are already home.

The Exhale of the Unmanaged Heart

THE AUDIT HAS BEEN CANCELLED. YOU DON'T HAVE TO mirror the ones who hurt you anymore. You don't have to be a sheriff to be safe. When you drop the badge, you don't fall into exile; you fall into the river.

The Hired Hand runs because he is tethered to the profit; the Shepherd stays because He is tethered to the Person. You are home, and you are allowed to be unmanaged. Letting go of the Hired Hand identity feels like dying because that badge was your only shield. But when the shield falls, the current takes you. You realize you don't have to become something to fit in; you simply have to be in One who has never once looked away.

The Shepherd does not manage the current; He *is* the current. When we stop trying to be the Sheriffs of His reputation, we discover that His reputation was never in danger. It was only our awareness that was at risk. The Father is not looking for a defense attorney; He is looking for a dinner guest. The shared life—the story, the tears, the laughter—is not the 'fluff' of the Kingdom; it is the very substance of the King. To be unmanaged is not to be chaotic; it is to be perfectly aligned with the only Heart that knows how to stay.

The End of the Scorecard: Shared Life

When the Father spoke about story, delight, tears, and laughter, He wasn't giving me a new communication style; He was giving me a new ontological rhythm. He revealed that the tributary doesn't carry a clipboard.

The church has, in many corners, forgotten who she is. She has behaved like a middle-manager, perpetually grappling for position and posturing for prominence, as if the Father's love were a limited resource that must be guarded by the most qualified among us. We have spent our energy fighting a defeated enemy and auditing the worthiness of our brothers, never realizing that Love—the very river we claim to represent—does not keep a record of wrong.

If the river doesn't keep a record, how can we? When we truly immerse ourselves in the Father, we lose the ability to keep score. We become unprofitable to the system of audit because we are no longer interested in the currency of debt. We possess a reckless, unmanaged abandon as we sit and love.

12

The Fruit Of Two Trees

The Binary Trap of "Good" and "Bad"

THERE IS A PROFOUND, QUIET EXHALE THAT HAP-
pens when you realize you no longer have to be
"good" to be loved. For many of us, the primary
vocabulary used to define our worth was not the language of
Relationship, but the language of the binary—the constant,
oscillating grading of 'Good' and 'Bad.' We have spent our lives
trying to eat from the branch of 'Good' to avoid the branch of
'Evil,' never realizing that both branches belong to the same
tree of exhaustion.

For many of us, the primary vocabulary used to define our
worth was not the language of relationships, but the language
of the binary—the constant, oscillating grading of good and
bad. Before we even knew who we were, we knew where we
stood on the scale.

Our actions encounter declarations that install a
courtroom in our developing minds from the moment we can
interpret a parent's smile or a teacher's scowl. We are a 'good
boy' for sharing our toys or a 'bad girl' for hitting our siblings.

On the surface, this looks like moral instruction. But underneath, we are being trained to manage our standing rather than our hearts.

We learn quickly that good equals connection and bad equals separation. The avoidance of bad stems from a fear of shame after judgment, not from a bond with Love. We aren't being moral; we are being protective. A defense fund of good deeds, essentially a spiritual savings account, is being quietly built by us to pay for the times our humanity inevitably surfaces, requiring us to buy back our favor. This is the exhausting architecture of the binary mind: a life spent not in love, but in litigation.

The Tale of Two Angies

I EXPERIENCED THE CUTTING POWER OF LABELING DURing my teenage years. By a quirk of fate and geography, I grew up with a friend who shared my name. The world, unable to handle the simplicity of two people sharing a name without a way to rank them, did what it always does: it chose the math of merit and assigned a verdict.

I was labeled "Good Angie." My friend was labeled "Bad Angie."

I remember a specific night that became a monument to the prison of being good. My friends had sneaked out of a sleepover. The air in the room was electric with the thrill of the forbidden. I wanted to go; I wanted to be part of the adventure. But I was a hostage to my own reputation, terrified of losing the reprieve my good label provided.

As the window creaked open and the last of them disappeared into the dark, they left me behind. I sat in that silent room, the clock ticking like a metronome in a courtroom. I wasn't being holy; I was being a hostage. It was in that quiet, lonely moment I realized that good Angie was just as much of a facade as any rebellion. The world saw my choice as a virtue, but for me, it was a cage. I was just as managed by the expectation of 'Good' as my friend was by the label of 'Bad.' Neither of us was free. This is the binary trap: the moment we agree with a label, we stop living from our nature and start living from a script. We see the ultimate anatomy of this trap in the land of Oz.

The Wizard of Measure: A Breakdown of Oz

THIS BINARY OBSESSION IS NOT JUST A TEENAGE struggle; it is the fundamental script of our most cherished cultural myths. We see the ultimate anatomy of this trap in the story of the land of Oz—a world that, on the surface, appears to be a pretty package of emeralds and sparkles but is governed by a hidden, transactional courtroom.

The *Wizard of Oz* has been a foundational geography of

my soul since I was a little girl. In my family, watching it every Thanksgiving was as much a liturgy as the turkey and the prayer. When I was ten years old, I lived the story from the inside, playing a Munchkin in a summer musical in the park. I knew the steps; I knew the songs, and I knew the rules of the road.

But recently, I found myself watching the forbidden flick, *Wicked*, tucked under a blanket in my living room. I approached it feeling like a literal rebel. Many religious voices warned people to stay away, claiming that they cast incantations and spells over those who dare to watch. But I couldn't help myself; this story had been part of my entire life, and I absolutely had to know the rest of the tale.

The epic retelling of the Oz narrative serves as a profound cultural case study for the very transactional courtroom we are dismantling. While many in the religious world have spent their energy guarding the gates against the perceived witchcraft of this story, they may have missed the fact that the Storyteller was using a green girl to whisper a higher truth about the Tree of Measure than most sermons or prophecies ever will.

For generations, the world was content with the surface-level verdict: Glinda was the good witch because she was blonde, bubbly, and wore a crown of sparkles. Elphaba was the wicked witch because she was green, misunderstood, and refused to comply with the status quo. I knew from the opening scene, as Glinda floated into Munchkin land in that sparkling, crystalline bubble, that this was more than a movie. It was an urgent prophecy about the perils of the wrong tree.

I sat there, a girl from Kansas hiding under a blanket, and realized that Glinda was the ultimate good Angie. She was blonde, bubbly, and wore a crown of compliance. She had traded her authentic friendship and her moral compass for a seat in a floating bubble and the applause of a mob. We have conditioned ourselves to envy Glinda. We want the crown, the sparkles, and the floating bubble that keeps us safely above the unwashed reality of the wreckage. But look closer at the bubble: it is the ultimate high place. To stay 'Good' in the eyes of the Wizard, Glinda had to accept a life of manicured isolation. The bubble doesn't just lift you up—it keeps you from touching anyone.

The sting hit me in the dark: Whether our familial line lands on extreme wickedness or brilliant goodness; it is still the same tree. A study in the wrong pursuit. Glinda became a Hired Hand for a fraudulent system, a prisoner of the 'Good' label, forced to maintain a shimmering facade while the Wizard systematically stripped the Animals of Oz of their voices and their rights. Her goodness was conditional—a performance exchanged for position.

Meanwhile, Elphaba's wickedness was actually her nature of integrity. They labeled her a villain not because she was evil, but because she refused to use the Scales. She saw the corruption behind the curtain and was indivisibly one with the truth, even if it cost her the limelight and her reputation. She realized that in a world governed by a fraudulent Wizard—that man with no actual power, managing a population through the optics of fear—being labeled good meant being a slave to a lie.

Her 'wickedness' was, in fact, her wholeness. I realized then that my own ministry excellence and my curated reputation were just my version of Glinda's bubble. I had been trying to stay elevated, terrified that if I touched the ground—if I let the blanket fall and showed the mess of my own sifting—I would lose my standing in the audit. But the Father isn't in the bubble with the Wizard. He's on the ground, in the mud, with the 'Wicked' girl who was brave enough to let the audit fail her so she could finally be free.

For a girl from Kansas, the realization is staggering: 'There's no place like home' was never about a dusty farmhouse or a physical destination. It was a prophetic whisper about the Porch. It's the soul's recognition that the audit is a foreign country, and the only place where we truly breathe is in the unmanaged, unmerited embrace of the Father. We don't have to click our heels to get there; we just have to realize we never actually left.

The Audit of the Kings: Good or Evil in His Sight

JUST AS WE MUST PULL BACK THE CURTAIN ON THE Wizard's binary of Good and Wicked in Oz, we must pull back the religious curtain on the Kings of Israel. For centuries, we have read their stories through a lens of measure, grading them like students on a curve. But God wasn't looking for a perfect report card; He was looking for the plumb line of alignment.

This binary obsession isn't just a cultural quirk; it runs so deep that we have projected it onto the very pages of Scripture. When we read the Chronicles of the Kings of Israel and Judah, we are confronted again and again by a resounding verdict: "He did what was good in the sight of the Lord," or "He did what was evil in the sight of the Lord." It reads, at first glance, like the ultimate spiritual report card—a heavenly audit with boxes to check and grades to assign.

Under the influence of the transactional system, we misinterpret these judgments as final scores on personal moral achievement. We imagine God with a clipboard, evaluating each king's record, separating the Strong Biblical Men from the failures. Many of us have inherited this lens, believing that

God's favor rides on performance, perfection, and unblemished fruit. Churches and families pass on this anxiety, teaching us to fear every slip, every rebellious shadow, lest we lose our place on the divine honor roll.

But a closer look at the Plumb Line reveals a divergence from this transactional logic. When we read that a King did evil in the sight of the Lord, our religious brain immediately scans for a moral scandal. We think he was a bad boy. But if you look at the architecture of their failure, evil was almost always defined by the construction of distance. They built high places. Beyond merely building altars; they were building moats. They were creating layers of bureaucracy, ritual, and performance to manage a God they were terrified to trust. They traded the face-to-face of the Porch for the tier-to-tier of the Temple.

Historians frequently describe Israel's monarchy as a moral seesaw, characterized by cycles of revival and subsequent decline into idolatry. We are told that King Asa or King Hezekiah *did what was right in the eyes of the Lord*. We applaud their reforms and their zeal. But look closer at the fine print of their stories: *Nevertheless, the high places were not removed.*

Even in their best seasons, they couldn't dismantle the high places—those internal altars where they still measured their worth by their performance. They were shimmering in the eyes of the people, but internally they were still slaves to the Scales. They were trying to be enough for a God they perceived as a demanding Auditor. The result was always the same: exhaustion, pride, or a final-act collapse into fear. They were willing to fix the kingdom, but they weren't quite ready to trust that they were already enough without the shimmering reputation of being a reformer.

The Proximal Heart of David

CONTRAST THIS WITH GOOD KING DAVID. BY ANY earthly metric, David should have failed the audit spectacularly. He broke commandments, shattered relationships, and left a wake of grief and disorder. He was a blood-stained disaster. But God called him a man after His own heart, not because David escaped failure, but because when failure came, he returned to the Source.

Again and again, David chose proximity to God's Presence over the pretense of his own goodness. He refused to build a moat. He came very close to being a disaster. He seemed to possess a cellular memory of the Father's knitting; a primal recognition of what it felt like to be held. When he failed, he didn't build an altar to bridge the gap; he simply fell into the Lap of the Father. He understood that the only important high place was the one where he sat. The evil Kings tried to bridge the distance; David lived as if the distance were a lie.

The High Places of the Adjective

THEN THERE IS SOLOMON—REVERED FOR HIS WISDOM, but eventually seduced by the delusion of self-sufficiency. Solomon's fall began not with some blatant public scandal, but with a quiet drift into the High Places of the Adjective. He became 'The Wise King,' 'The Builder,' 'The Wealthy.' These titles became his bubble of manicured isolation. His temple became crowded out by high places—literal and metaphorical altars of compromise erected to maintain his shimmering status. The binary verdict of good or evil was never really about untainted records; it was always a mirror of whether hearts remained open to the river or built dams in the name of control.

In modern times, our High Places emerge as denominational pride, doctrinal gatekeeping, or the High Places of the Adjective. We hide our naked sonship behind titles like 'Strong Leader' or 'Anointed Vessel,' believing we must earn access again and again.

But the Father isn't interested in the structural integrity of your high place. He is looking to level it, so that the river of His delight can finally flow over the ruins of your efforts and carry you back to the chair He already pulled out for you. David's life offers us a counter-narrative, not of moral management, but of relational return. This is where the metaphor of the Tree of Life pushes us beyond the Accounting of Merits. The Tree of Life invites us, instead, to permanent, unmediated connection—life as a branch united to the Vine, letting fruit be the overflow, not the obsession. Today, our challenge is to live as people of alignment, not as auditors. Are you busy managing your fruit, counting good days and bad? Or are you living proximally, present to the river?

Let the life of David, with all his mess and mercy, be an invitation: God's question was never, 'Did you keep your report card clean?' It was, 'Did you come back to Me?' The Tree of Life stands open, inviting you out of the exhausting courtroom of audit and into the sanctuary of Presence. Which tree will you choose?

Moving from Measure to Abiding

JESUS DIDN'T JUST COME TO TIP THE SCALES IN OUR favor; He came to smash the machine entirely. He shattered this binary trap by taking the place of the bad one. In a moment of supreme subversion, He stood where a criminal should have stood and He revealed that the Father's justice isn't about managing the spectrum of good and evil—it's about pulling us out of that entire system and replanting us into the Tree of Life.

When we shift our residence to the Tree of Life, the definitions change. We are no longer defined by our moral performance—our fluctuating stock price of good days and bad days—but by our nature in Him. To live from this place means we must consciously, and sometimes violently, stop the internal audit. We have to fire the accountant in our heads.

I spent years attempting to maintain high places in my own soul—standards of performance and layers of religious mediation that I believed kept me close to God. I invested my identity in titles and roles, believing that my standing was something to be managed. But I realized that a high place is just a fancy name for a barricade. It is a structure we erect to manage a distance that doesn't actually exist. We stop asking if we were productive or holy enough today and start asking the only question that matters: Are we abiding?

This shift changes everything. Our focus moves from the quality of the grape to the health of the connection. In the agricultural reality of the Kingdom, the branch doesn't strain or sweat to produce fruit; it simply stays connected to the Vine. We trust the flow of the Spirit, realizing that our character, our peace, and our kindness are not products we manufacture on an assembly line, but the natural, inevitable overflow of the

Vine's life surging through us. You don't have to 'try' to grow a grape; you just have to stay attached.

Finally, we are free to just be children on the Porch. We stop saying pardon me for our humanity and start reveling in the life that is flowing through us. We realize that the Father isn't looking for a polished presentation; He's looking for a living relationship. Love is messy, organic, and unmeasured—and the Father likes it that way.

The moment we stop measuring our lives, the 'good mask' falls off, and the 'bad one' dissolves. Finally, we are free to just be children on the Porch. We stop saying 'pardon me' for our humanity and start reveling in the life that is flowing through us. We realize that the Father isn't looking for a polished presentation; He's looking for a living relationship. Love is messy, organic, and unmeasured—and the Father likes it that way.

If the Courtroom of the Calculated Worth is defined by an audit, a feast defines the Father's Porch. One of the most profound struggles for a heart transitioning from the plantation of performance to the freedom of the Porch is the simple inability to enjoy. For so long, our training in a scarcity mindset has led us to view joy as an indulgence we haven't quite earned, a luxury item on a menu we cannot afford. We approach the Lord's table expecting a price list, like in a cafeteria, instead of a banquet where someone settled the bill before we arrived.

Living from your foundation means you will transition from a contractor that just consumes earnings to a son that eats due to love. It means believing that your seat at the table is secured not by your good behavior, but by your bloodline as a child of God. But as I learned on a quiet afternoon during a season of deep family service, sometimes the hardest part of the feast isn't receiving the food; it's being asked to make a place at the table for those who represent your deepest pain.

13
The Sovereignty Of The Chair

I F THE FATHER LIKES THE MESS, THEN WHY DO WE spend so much energy trying to hide our crumbs? For years, I believed that 'messy' meant 'disqualified.' I understood the theology of the Tree of Life, but I was still spiritually squatting on the floor. I didn't realize how much I preferred the shadows until the King reached for the tablecloth.

There are encounters that don't just happen to you; they become the geography you live in. For over a decade, this vision has been the plumb line I return to whenever the "Audit" tries to call me back to the floor. It is the story that finally identified the orphan hiding in my own bones.

I didn't realize how much I preferred the shadows until the King reached for the tablecloth.

I had navigated my spiritual life with a brand of humility that looked holy on the outside but felt like a hiding place on the inside. In a moment of deep prayer, I found myself in a vision. I was a little girl, small and quiet, tucked away in the darkness beneath a massive white banquet table. The fabric of the tablecloth was heavy and thick—a cotton shroud that separated me from the light of the room.

I was perfectly content there. I wasn't protesting the floor; I was embracing it. I lived on the scraps and the crumbs that fell from above, believing that my unseen status was a form of safety. I thought that by staying under the table; I was avoiding being seen. They couldn't grade my manners if I wasn't at the table. If I hid, people couldn't find me lacking.

But then, the corner of the cloth was pulled back.

A hand reached down—not to point a finger of correction, but to offer a gesture of total inclusion. Jesus leaned over, pulled the corner of the fabric aside, and looked me directly in the eyes. His gaze was kind, yet it carried an unwavering authority. He didn't ask me to clean up so I could earn a seat; He simply pulled the chair out beside Him and summoned me higher.

As I climbed out from the shadows and onto that chair, the world expanded. I realized the table wasn't a small, exclusive VIP booth. It was a landscape. The table stretched for miles in every direction, occupied by a vast cloud of witnesses, each plate holding a feast that differed from person to person. There was a copious amount of food and drink, an abundance that made my scraps look like the tragedy they were.

As I turned to look into Christ's eyes, I saw something

that shattered my religious definitions of God. I didn't see a stern judge or a distant king; I saw a profound, lingering Sorrow.

It was a holy grief that emanated from Him—not because I had been 'bad,' but because He had so deeply longed for me to share the seat beside Him. I realized in that gaze that my 'humility' was actually a barrier to His joy. He considered it backhanded for me to remain on that floor, content with scraps, while He had authored my place at the table before the world began. Staying under the tablecloth wasn't modesty; it was the active maintenance of an orphan heart that refused to be wooed.

But my delight swallowed the moment I settled into that chair. I wasn't met with a lecture on my tardiness; I was met with a surge of joy that felt like air finally hitting my lungs after a long dive. The 'scraps' didn't just seem small; they became non-existent. The Feast's light made me realize with staggering certainty that I was exactly where I was always meant to be.

I didn't know then that this seat was more than a place of rest. It was a place of preparation. The King hadn't moved me to the chair just so I could eat; He moved me there so I could see the guests He would invite into my story.

This vision was not a one time ticket out of my insecurity; it became the land I inhabit. In the fourteen years since that afternoon, I have returned to this table repeatedly. Whenever the audit screams or the weight of a new trial makes me feel small, I don't look for a new revelation. I simply go back to the chair He pulled out for me. I close my eyes and remember the weight of the cotton cloth, the kindness in His gaze, and the miles of copious feasting that prove there is no scarcity in His house. The table is where I remember who I am when the world tries to tell me I'm still just a girl looking for scraps.

The Bed of the Adversary: The Weight of the Linens

It was this habit of returning to the table that sustained me when the most troublesome guests arrived. Because I knew the scale of the miles of feast, I knew I didn't have to protect my own plate—even when the seating chart felt like a violation.

In a season marked by caretaking and quiet service, the low-grade fever of anxiety I thought I had finally mastered spiked. The phone rang with a request that felt like a final breaking of the heart: The parents of the man who had violated our daughters were coming to visit.

They weren't coming to see us; they were coming to visit my mother-in-law. They had lived behind a wall of desperate silence; perhaps a reality they weren't prepared to inhabit shielded them. I can understand the shattering reflex to defend— the instinct that led them to shield their son while accusing our daughters of lying. It wasn't because they loved crime, but because they couldn't survive the loss of knowledge.

However, our intertwined lives made their presence an unavoidable collision. My mother-in-law asked if I was genuinely concerned about their arrival as the date drew closer. In that moment, I decided it was time to stop pretending. I reached down and lifted the corner of the rug that she had used to sweep the horrifying details under. I didn't just tell her I was bothered; I exposed the jagged edges of the wreckage. I let her see the mess that her denial had only prolonged.

The room grew cold. My mother-in-law looked at me, and instead of meeting the truth I had finally uncovered with a hand of comfort, she met it with a demand of duty: "I need you to go strip and make their bed for them."

I walked away in disbelief, stealing a moment to grieve alone. To provide comfort for the lineage that had produced our nightmare? It felt like a betrayal of my own children. It felt like I was being asked to subsidize my own trauma with my labor while the truth remained unacknowledged. The injustice of it choked me. A collision between her desperate need for hollow decorum and my desperate need for recognition trapped me.

But as I sat in the debris of my own spirit, God met me. He didn't give me a lecture on religious duty. He simply asked one question that pierced through the noise of my wounds: "Will you do it for Me?"

I went into that guest room, and I did it. I remember the weight of the linens in my hands—how heavy and cold the cotton felt against my skin. I realized with sickening clarity that I was smoothing the very fabric where our nightmare had its roots. While the worst of his intentions had been intercepted before they could reach our daughters, the shadow of what he had planned, sat heavy on that mattress. I wasn't just making a bed; I was working the ground where he had hoped to bury their innocence.

It felt like proof I was still so broken, so vulnerable. Every tucked corner was a reminder of what we had nearly lost. But as I tucked those corners, Jesus was beckoning me deeper. He was showing me that my act of service wasn't a submission to a defensive family dynamic; it was a submission to the river.

As I smoothed the fabric, I realized I wasn't alone in that room. He was there all along, holding the other end of the sheet and untangling the tightened fear in my heart. It was the proximal Kindness of the Father that kept me from drowning. In that moment, the river wasn't a metaphor; it was the only way I could breathe. I had to know that God wasn't just nice; I had to know He was just, and that His justice was a restorative force big enough to handle the wreckage I was touching.

This is the feasting nature of Being: the ability to set a table in the presence of an enemy—realizing that in the light of the Cross, even the enemy is a sibling caught in the same weary fog that still has the ability to blind you. You aren't ignoring the debt; you are standing in a river where the King swallowed the debt whole. To feast in their presence is to declare that Christ's sacrifice is large enough to cover the wreckage between you, transforming a battleground into a shared inheritance. I had to find out the next day if I actually believed that the grace which secured my seat was the same grace securing theirs.

The Kitchen Table Bridge

BECAUSE THEY WERE GUESTS IN THE HOUSE, THE VISIT BEcame a study in the shadow and light.

Initially, the air in the room felt heavy, like a conversation looking for a place to land. Even though he was there for a family visit, the father of the man seemed caught in a restless, circling momentum around the wound. Not that he was seeking to cause more pain; he seemed to search for a version of the truth that his own heart could survive—a way to reconcile the son of his pride with the man of the nightmare. I could feel the vulture mentality at work—not as a predator, but as a desperate survival instinct, hungry for any weakness in the story that might offer him a reprieve from the devastating reality. He was a sibling still shadowboxing a world that he felt was closing in on him.

Feeling the familiar pressure of that defense attempt to rise in my own chest, I walked away. I threw my food in the trash and left the room. I refused to let my own heart be drawn back into a trial the Father had already moved past.

The mother—the sister my mother-in-law was hosting—approached me. She didn't come with the heavy gavel of her husband's defense. By her posture, she showed a preference for the relationship over the script while engaging in a quiet conversation about ordinary things. She didn't solve the tragedy; she simply shared the space. She acted as a shepherd of the quiet, guarding the small patch of clear air we were standing on so that the fog had nowhere to land.

A bridge spanned the chasm of horrific pain in that moment. We weren't characters in a legal brief or players in a family drama. We were just two siblings sitting at a table that neither of us had to build. Grace, served at a kitchen table, dissolved the tension, not through debate of the truth, but by its presence.

This is the practical reality of the Porch: True restoration doesn't begin with a verdict; it begins with a safe place to sit down. When you refuse to play the role of the defendant, the courtroom loses its jurisdiction, even when the spirit of the judge is sleeping in the next room.

The Older Brother's Fast

RETURNING TO THE SCENE OF THE FEAST, WE FIND THAT the climax of the story isn't the younger son's repentance or his long walk home. The Father doesn't just offer a pardon; he offers a party. He doesn't just restore the son's position; he celebrates his presence. But while the music plays and the fattened calf is served, the Older Brother remains outside in the field, angry and refusing to enter.

This is the great tragedy of the religious mind, a heart conditioned by transactional math: It cannot handle a joy it did not manage. To the hired-hand mentality, a feast for the undeserving is an injustice. The older brother believes his father's love is a limited resource, a reward to be earned through dutiful service. From his perspective, the celebration is an insult to his hard work and moral superiority. He is fasting out of spite, trapped in a self-imposed hunger strike because he refuses to acknowledge a justice that is restorative rather than retributive.

When we refuse to enjoy life, the Father has given us—or when we refuse to let the river of His grace flow toward those who have hurt us—we are standing in that same field, missing the music from the Porch. The older brother couldn't stomach the feast for the same reason the crowd in Jerusalem chose Barabbas: he couldn't handle unmerited grace for the undeserving. In his transactional world, the criminal should be on the execution platform, not at the head of the table. He is so busy auditing the guest list that he misses the Host. The great irony is that the Father's feast was for him, too, but his sense of entitlement became the very fence that kept him out.

The Feasting Ontology

WHEN YOU SIT AT THE FATHER'S TABLE, EVEN WHEN ENemies surround it, God pulls you from the courtroom and places you at the center of the Divine Dance. This is the feasting nature: a profound, bedrock realization that your presence at the table is the very thing the Father desired before the foundation of the world. Your invitation isn't a reward; it's a homecoming.

Practicing this in a system that still wants to audit us requires a radical, moment-by-moment shift. We must learn to stop the relentless self-audit at the door of our hearts. We must begin to see acts of service not as obligations but as declarations of sovereignty. Making the bed for those who have hurt you isn't being a doormat; it is a profound act of war against the scales. You prove that your peace is not for sale, your joy is not contingent, and their actions or opinions do not manage your identity. A deeper reality anchors you.

Feasting is the active recognition that the Father is currently, actively, and joyfully delighted in you, regardless of who else is sitting at the table. The Porch is not a place of potential or a future reward for good behavior; it is a place of Presence. It is the here-and-now reality for every child of God. The table is ready. The music is playing, and the Father is holding your chair, waiting for you to sit down and receive.

The audition is over. The feast has begun.

PART IV
THE RHYTHM OF RESTORATION

The courtroom doors are locked from the inside. The Hired Hand has been evicted, and the binary ledgers of good and evil have been tossed. What remains is not a project to be completed, but a life to be lived.

The table is set, and the seating chart is simple: you are already in. We aren't here to earn the feast, but to take part in the Divine Dance that has been spinning since before time began. It is time to drop the weight of the debt and finally taste what happens when the leaking smile of the Father becomes the only rhythm your heart needs to follow.

14

The Leaking Smile

> Perichoresis: The Divine Dance. The eternal, joyful, reciprocal indwelling of the Father, Son, and Holy Spirit. You are not a spectator; you are a participant.

> The Oxytocin Lock: The biological result of love-based bonding. Unlike the adrenaline of fear, this is the chemical of attachment that quiets the nervous system and allows the soul to rest in the Indivisibly One reality.

Worship, Oxytocin, and the Mud Vats

THE EXHAUSTION WE CARRY IS FED BY THE SPIRitual content we consume. For many of us, the act of singing on a Sunday morning has become a taxing ritual—a hidden labor where we unconsciously work to maintain a contract we no longer need. We treat lyrics like background noise, but they are actually a liturgy of the soul. They are the catechism of the heart, shaping our fundamental identity and our view of God. To truly live in reconciliation, we must understand the core truth we are bonding with, for we cannot rest in a Father we are secretly singing against. If the music reinforces the distance, then the Porch remains a theoretical concept rather than a lived reality.

The Sunday Script: Worship as a Weighted Ritual

WHEN THE SONGS WE SING EMPHASIZE A CHASM BETWEEN us and the Divine, or suggest that our worth is a fluctuating currency based on our morning's behavior, we are being trained in the courtroom's theology. We are acting like tenants who are still paying rent on a house that the Father already gave us as an inheritance. Every "Lord, come down" is a subtle denial of "It is finished." We are trying to build a bridge that Christ already built. This weighted ritual keeps us in the Mud Vats of religious effort, where we measure the success of our worship by the level of our own exhaustion.

The Hot Tear: The Day the Song Broke

I REMEMBER A MORNING SEVERAL SEASONS AGO. I WAS standing in a large worship gathering, the kind with professional lighting and a sound system so powerful it vibrated in your very marrow. The room was agreeing with a popular anthem; dozens of hands raised in the collective roar of the crowd. Then, the bridge of the song arrived. The lyrics scrolled across the screen in a bold, undeniable font: "The Father turned His face away."

The statement struck me with the force of a physical blow. I stopped singing mid-syllable. My hands, raised in a reflex of compliance, dropped heavily to my sides. I stood there in total dismay, a heavy, cold weight settling in my stomach like lead. While the surrounding room swelled with emotion, a single, hot tear rolled down my cheek—not out of worship, but out of a profound, spiritual grief.

That lyric was asking me to stand on Pilate's pavement again. It was asking me to believe that in the moment of ultimate union—the moment Christ bore our wreckage—the Trinity fractured. It presented a Father who is so holy He cannot look upon sin, which means He cannot look upon me the moment I stumble. If He could turn away from Jesus—the perfect, beloved Son—the whisper of the older brother in my heart said He would certainly turn away from me.

If the Father turned away from the Son, then the distance is real, and the kiss of justice was actually a blow of rejection. I would be back on the platform, one mistake away from abandonment, desperately trying to be good enough to keep the

Father's face toward me. But I knew in my gut it could not be true. The truth is fiercer and more beautiful: The Father was *in* Christ, reconciling the world to Himself.

The Phenomenal Encounter: The Liturgy of the Breast

IN THAT MOMENT OF HEARTBREAK, THE HOLY SPIRIT whisked me away into an encounter. The roar of the worship band faded, and the Holy Spirit showed me the true dynamic of what transpires in the spirit during a moment of union. He revealed to me that worship is not an ascent to reach a far-off deity; it is a biological and spiritual bonding.

As a mother who nursed all six of my babies, I have lived this liturgy thousands of times. I know the quiet hours of the middle-of-the-night vigils when the rest of the house is a tomb of silence and the world outside feels non-existent. In those early days, the relationship is one of pure, raw necessity. The heavy rhythm of provision and the desperate, instinctive reception of what is offered satisfies this need. You are the source, and they are the need.

But as the days turn into weeks, the encounter shifts from a transaction of calories to a phenomenon of mutual recognition. I can still recall the weight of a tiny, restless head in the crook of my arm—that heavy, trusting settling that happens the moment skin touches skin. It is a biological click, resting into the foundation where the child realizes they are no longer searching.

I remember the specific moments when my babies became more interactive, moving beyond the reflexive need for milk into the intentionality of connection. They would stop mid-feed, small hands resting against my chest, and lock eyes with mine. It was a gaze so intense it felt as if they were drinking in my very identity. They were not looking for a portal to their mother; they were resting in the habitation of her arms.

In that stillness, something extraordinary would happen. The sheer, staggering joy of belonging, the knowledge that they were wanted, would overwhelm them, causing a grin to break across their face. It was a smile of unadulterated delight. It was so sudden and so large that they could not contain the milk they had just received; it would leak through their joy and onto my midsection. They were literally overflowing with the satisfaction of being home.

This is the root of the name *El Shaddai*. The Hebrew root *shad* refers to the breast—the ultimate source of nourishment and protection. In this state, the mother and child co-regulate. My peace was becoming their peace; my strength was becoming their floor. This true worship looks like: the leaking smile of a child who realizes they do not have to achieve the mother; they already possess her.

Adrenaline vs. Oxytocin: The Biology of the Amen

STANDING IN THAT SERVICE, I REALIZED THAT FOR CENturies, the religious system has been fear-bonding us with God. When we sing songs filled with language about wrath, separation, or a face turned away, our bodies release adrenaline—the fight-or-flight hormone. Adrenaline forces us into a posture of vigilance. Over time, this kind of worship leaves people with a chronic sense of spiritual anxiety, convincing them that God's nearness is fragile and that they must continually earn it. The result is a trauma bond with the divine: we stay close to God not because we trust His embrace, but because we fear the consequences of distance.

Therefore, I find it difficult to stomach worship songs that put God up there—high, unreachable, and surrounded by angels while we stand on the outside looking in. This language isn't just poetic; it's a rift. It defaults to a televised faith where the genuine encounter is for someone else, somewhere else. It trains our anatomy to believe the lie of separation.

The contrast is stark when we encounter love-bonding. When worship arises from the bedrock of secured reconciliation—when praise declares that we are already home—the brain releases oxytocin. Known as the bonding molecule, oxytocin engenders trust, contentment, and a deep sense of belonging. If adrenaline carves worry, oxytocin carves rest. This shift changes the very nature of our Amen. We aren't singing for access; we are singing from the center of the circle. We move from petitioning a landlord to taking part in the dance of a Father—and a Mother. The best litmus test for worship is not how exhausted it leaves us, but whether it roots us deeper in the rest Christ has already won.

The New Liturgy: The Trust Factor

STANDING THERE WITH THAT HOT TEAR ON MY CHEEK, I realized the Father had finally resolved the very thing He had diagnosed years ago on that country road. Back then, surrounded by crowned corn that rustled like dry parchment, He had spoken the words that started this entire journey: "You don't trust me!"

In the cornfield, it was a hard truth I had to face. But here, in the light of the finished work, it became the key to my freedom. I finally understood that intimacy is directly proportional to surrender. If we hold back, trying to manage our own justice or protect our own reputation, we stay locked in the courtroom. Trust is simply the act of letting go of the Audit and falling into the arms of the Father.

The new liturgy of the reconciled heart rejects any language of separation. It refuses to sing of a Father who turns

His face away, because it knows that the Godhead is indivisible. We no longer sing to bridge a gap; we sing to celebrate a Union. Our praise is the joyful, oxytocin-fueled affirmation of who we already are—an indivisible branch resting securely in the Vine.

The Father is not turning His face away; He is leaning in, waiting for that leaking smile to break across your face. He isn't waiting for you to get it right; He is waiting for you to realize He already has. This is the end of the Audit. This is the beginning of Life.

15

The Mission: Let Justice Roll

The River's Mission

A LIFE THAT IS FULL EVENTUALLY LEAKS. THE FEAST we've enjoyed on the Porch was never intended to be a private luxury; it is a pressurized grace that eventually breaks its banks. We don't 'go' on a mission; we simply stop holding back the river.

The feast is not the end of the story; it is the beginning of the mission. As we rise from the table, satiated by the Father's acceptance, we carry the atmosphere of the Porch into a world desperate for the river's flow. This is the river's Mission: to let the grace we've received become the grace we give.

The victory of the Cross was not merely for your personal peace; it was the definitive act that birthed a mission. You have undergone a fundamental shift in your spiritual Biology because the Father's porch wooed you home. You are no longer defined by where you are going or what you are achieving; you are defined by what is flowing through you. To be indivisibly one is to be a living tributary of the river of reconciliation. This river is wild and sovereign. It doesn't respect fences, religious protocols, or the Do Not Disturb signs of our personal comfort. It flows out from a secure identity into a world that is desperately, dangerously thirsty for restorative justice. We naturally and inevitably overflow with this mission due to our new nature: Christ reconciled us to God, and now we simply carry that atmosphere into every room we enter. We become mobile sanctuaries, leaking the Father's presence into the dry ground of a broken world.

The Barabbas Exchange as the Mission

BARABBAS, IN THE STORY, IS NOT JUST A MAN—HE IS THE embodied delusion of separation, the echo of who we thought we were in Adam: distant, disqualified, and unworthy. We have all worn that name, believing ourselves estranged from the Father, haunted by the courtroom's verdict. Yet, while we stood on the platform cloaked in shame and confusion, the Father's heart remained unmoved by our delusion. His gaze remained fixed on us—not with disappointment, but with the full, unstoppable reality of our belonging.

At the cross, Jesus did not simply take the place of a single prisoner. He shattered the myth of distance for all humanity. He absorbed every lie of alienation, every vestige of Adam's shame, and in that decisive act, the Judge became the Father running toward Barabbas; not to reprimand or restrict, but to embrace and restore. The Barabbas exchange is the moment the illusion of separation met its end; the platform of shame is now empty, the cell of condemnation is unlocked, and the Father stands waiting on the Porch, already convinced of our inclusion.

This, then, is our mission: to live from the truth that the debt of separation is gone and to confront the lie of distance wherever we find it—in ourselves and in others. Our lives become living announcements, reminding the weary and the wandering that the Father runs toward them with the fullness of His delight. We don't traffic in the logic of merit-based scales, demanding worth or meting out relational exile. We release, we feast, we welcome, because God has already made the payment and has never revoked the offer of home. When we love unconditionally, we echo the heart of the Father, One who refused to honor the delusion of separation and who still runs, arms open, to every son He sees.

The Two Voices of Justice: A Field Guide

THE GREATEST CHALLENGE IN LIVING THIS MISSION IS the constant, cacophonous background noise of the world. The world saturates us with the voice of transactional math— the zero-sum game of debt and payment. This voice is loud, aggressive, and culturally celebrated. It is the voice of getting what you deserve and making them pay. It is the algorithm of the news cycle and the default setting of our unhealed egos.

In contrast, the voice of the river—the constant, nourishing flow of *Chesed* (Mercy) and *Mishpat* (Justice)—is quieter. It does not scream for attention because it does not need to justify its existence. Tuning into this frequency requires the deliberate practice of rest. You cannot hear the river while you are running on the treadmill of performance.

When we default to the Ledger, our governing principles become retribution, debt, and exclusion. The ultimate outcome is always punishment—a form of justice that seeks to make things pay. When we operate from the old system, we are merely administering the same spiritual violence we once endured. We become vultures, circling the failures of others to feel better about our own fragile status. We feed on the carcass of someone else's mistake to nourish our own internal scrutiny.

Conversely, when we operate from the river voice, our governing principles shift to restoration, wholeness, and inclusion. The ultimate outcome is redemption—a justice that seeks to make things whole. We stop asking, 'Who is to blame?' and start asking, 'Where is the wound?' We cease to be inspectors of fruit, obsessively categorizing the rotten apples, and become healers of the soil, tending to the root systems where life actually begins.

The Secular Sanctuary: Where Ontology Breathes

ONE OF THE GREAT IRONIES OF THIS LIFE IS THAT OUR true nature—the one saturated with the peace of the porch — often breathes more easily in the secular domain than in the sacred. In the unfiltered world, people are frequently more honest about their wreckage. There is a baseline of humanity that isn't choked by the need to maintain religious reputations or perform spiritual adequacy.

Carrying the quiet authority of your original design draws people to you when you enter a boardroom, a gym, or a grocery store. Why? Because it is innocent. It has no agenda. It doesn't have an accounting hidden in its pocket or a conversion metric attached to its kindness. In the high-pressure environment of many religious systems, everyone is often shadowboxing, protecting their own standing and guarding against perceived threats to their righteousness.

But out in the world, the light of your settled identity shines without the interference of religious static. The river of grace flows more easily through the authentic cracks of a broken world than it does through the smooth, impenetrable concrete of a legalistic system. In places where no one is pretending to have it all together, the simple presence of someone who is truly at peace can feel like a sanctuary. Your rest becomes a revelation, and your unconditional acceptance becomes a quiet revolution against the world's relentless demand for performance.

Taking Relational Eviction Off the Table

This revolution begins at the center of our most intimate circles. Finally, we must live the mission by taking relational eviction off the table. We often think of justice as a series of calculated consequences, believing that if we do not withdraw our warmth, the offender will never learn the weight of their error. But the deepest consequence a human can feel —whether they are a spouse, a friend, or a child—isn't the loss of a privilege or a possession; it's the sudden, terrifying withdrawal of love.

Relational eviction is the ultimate tool of the Scales. This lie suggests that love can be a strategic weapon for punishing behavior. When a system relegates or silences a person, it is a tactical isolation designed to bring someone back into compliance through the threat of loneliness. It whispers,"Your safety depends on your usefulness," or "Your loved ones only accept your agreement."

But the mission of the river is to offer a non-withdrawable love. This means the people in our lives know that while we may address their behavior, their belonging is an immutable fact. We provide a safe harbor where the statute of limitations on their mistakes has already expired. When we take the threat of eviction off the table, we provide the only atmosphere where true transformation can actually happen. Fear may produce compliance, but only safety produces change.

We aren't just being nice or permissive; we are modeling the Father on the Porch, who never stopped watching the road, even while the son was still in the far country squandering his inheritance. He didn't wait for the apology to run. Before throwing the robe, he failed to check the ledger. He offered the embrace first because he knew that belonging is the soil in which transformation grows. By anchoring our relationships in this kind of security, we stop being judges guarding a courtroom and start being fathers and mothers tending a home.

Years after our own world had been dismantled, I sat in a jury box and most clearly felt the weight of this architectural shift. As the technicalities of a different trial unfolded before me, a staggering chronological fact struck me: the statute of limitations for our own family's trauma was ending. The window the world provides for its specific brand of retribution expired that very month—perhaps even that very day.

While we had long ago chosen to protect our daughters from the secondary violation of a legal proceeding, the timing of my presence in that courtroom felt orchestrated. I was being pulled back into the atmosphere of the Audit one last time, not to re-open a case, but to witness the boundary of the world's power. At the time, that ticking clock felt like the final closing of a door to fairness. But from the Porch, the view is different. The Father didn't just let the clock run out on my right to litigate; He revealed that in His Kingdom, the case had been dismissed for two thousand years.

The audit of your shame hasn't just expired because time passed; it has expired because the jurisdiction changed. The world's courtroom can only prosecute a nature that no longer exists. You cannot serve a summons on a new creation. The legal briefs you've been carrying are papers for a trial that was canceled long ago. The Judge has left the bench, courthouse staff have turned off the lights, and the only limit left is the limitless horizon of His delight.

The Final Verdict is a Homecoming

THE JOURNEY OF THIS BOOK HAS BEEN BOTH A DEMOLI-tion and a reconstruction. We have traced our spiritual exhaustion back to its source and found not a courtroom, but a home. We have dismantled the framework of performance and discovered that the Judge is, in truth, a Father. Because the Kiss of Justice was the decisive act of the Godhead, settling the issue of sin by exhausting its claim on us through the conquering power of love, we have proven that the Debt is Zero, not because we earned a pardon.

But to truly live on the Porch, we must finally abandon the function. For too long, many of our religious structures have operated from the strength of a fallen nature, even while preaching a risen Christ. We see it when a leader's mission results in injury to the very people they are called to serve—when the management of critics becomes a defensive shield, wielding the power of a gavel to protect a reputation rather than the vulnerability of the Porch to protect a child. This is the fruit of leading from a place of perceived lack.

Here is the staggering truth we must embrace: Christ covered us long before Adam made us fall. Our original identity is not one of separation but of divine inclusion. If we lead or live with the belief that we are still fundamentally fallen, we produce a murky result. The jaded lens of all has fallen short; clouds our perception of the world, preventing us from grasping the liberating reality that Christ securely holds everyone. The Son's job—and our job as living tributaries of the river— is singular: to reveal the In-Christ nature of everyone we meet. We are not here to expose sin, but to uncover the Son.

The Treasure Hunt of Sonship

WHEN LEADERSHIP HAPPENS WITHOUT A GENUINE HEART

of service—when it's merely a role we play rather than an over-flow of who we are—it creates a mirage. It offers the promise of water but delivers only sand. This kind of performance-based leadership inevitably requires triage for those left injured in its wake. A leader operating solely from function is often desperate to find footing, attaching their identity to titles, past trauma, or the compliance of their followers. They need you to need them, and that need becomes a heavy chain.

But I have encountered the sweet spot of the Porch in the form of a loyal son. In this encounter, the function—whether prophetic, pastoral, or apostolic—is seamless because it is the son you meet first. There is no fronting, no peacocking, and no desperate performance for validation. The atmosphere is clear. He only has eyes for who you are in Christ.

This kind of leader is on a perpetual treasure hunt with you. He is not looking for dirt; he is prospecting for gold. He seeks to qualify your personhood rather than quantify your utility. His open arms suggest welcome and restoration, as he stands just beyond the threshold, creating the illusion of no barrier. He isn't weighing your fruit on the merit-based math; he is celebrating your roots in the river.

This is the freedom of Sonship: the ability to pull the best from a person and display it before them convincingly, not as flattery, but because that is who they genuinely are. When you are secure in your own sonship, you don't need to diminish others to feel tall. You become a mirror reflecting the Father's face, showing people the beauty they possess but have forgotten how to see.

The Stone Platform and the Wooden Porch

WE BEGAN THIS JOURNEY ON A STONE PLATFORM, WITH A mob roaring for blood. The air was thick with the metallic scent of fear and the collective desperation of a people who believed the only way to be free was to watch someone else pay. Two figures stood before the crowd: one who represented the familiar logic of insurrection, and one who embodied the unsettling logic of love. Pilate asked the question that would echo through eternity: "Which one do you want me to release?"

The crowd chose the bandit. They chose the math of debt over the river, the sword over the embrace. They chose the familiar mechanism of retribution because they were terrified of a grace they couldn't control or predict. That cold stone platform represents the world's system of justice. In this place, people transact, feel fear, and perform, debating worth and granting freedom only if conditions are met.

But there is another place. It is a simple wooden Porch, worn smooth by the pacing of a patient Father. The air here is not thick with fear, but with the scent of a homecoming feast.

This is the place of grace, inclusion, and the river's unstoppable justice. On the Porch, your value isn't up for debate. Your belonging is never in question.

Here, at the end of this journey, you are being asked the same question: Which one do you choose?

Do you choose the stone platform—the exhausting, noble effort to balance your own accounts? Do you choose the system of debt, payment, and the perpetual audit of your own heart? Or do you choose the King who took the rebel's place? Do you choose the wooden Porch? Do you choose the justice that runs toward you before you've rehearsed your apology, that throws a feast while your hands are still dirty from the far country, and that seats you at the table not as a guest, but as a son?

The audition is over. The platform is empty. God rolled the stone away. The verdict on your life has already arrived, and it's a word the courtroom couldn't translate: Homecoming.

Wounded No More

I CAN TELL YOU FROM THE OTHER SIDE OF MY OWN SIFTing: Wounded No More is not just a hopeful declaration—it is a destination you can actually reach. It is a land you can inhabit.

Reclaiming your voice after challenges, silencing, or denial does not involve climbing a self-improvement ladder. It is simply about returning to the simple, foundational mandate of love. What we lack, the trauma we have endured, or the systems that oppose us do not define us. Our identity stems from the perfect, finished work, which places us at the right hand of the Father, far beyond any accusation or audit.

The Father does not do performance reviews. He only holds. Center isn't a destination you have to strive for; Center is the arms you are already in. You do not have to navigate His disappointment, because His disappointment in you does not exist. He isn't looking at you history of failures or successes; He is looking at His Son, and in Him, you are complete.

The statute of limitations on your shame has expired. The Father is not waiting for your perfection; He is simply waiting for you to embrace your rest. He has left the light on, and He is scanning the horizon, not for a servant returning to work, but for a child coming home. Justice isn't a cold stone platform where you wait in suspense; it's the living river that draws you home. Its current invites you to the table, not to prove yourself, but to discover what's already true in Christ.

The Unexpected Precedent: The Isaiah 61 Reality

BUT THIS INVITATION IS NOT A PRIVATE LUXURY. IF THE river is truly wild and sovereign, our own healing cannot contain it. It must eventually break its banks and flow into the lives of those the world has given up on. Lately, the Father has been proving this by setting a new, unexpected precedent in my own life. On the porch of my daily mission, a strange and beautiful gathering is taking place. The ones that religious systems have deemed "unfixable"—the prisoner, the unhomed, even the child abuser—are all finding their way to the water.

This is nothing short of an Isaiah 61 story unfolding in real-time:

> *The Spirit of the Sovereign Lord is on me, because the Lord has anointed me to proclaim good news to the poor. He has sent me to bind up the brokenhearted, to proclaim freedom for the captives and release from darkness for the prisoners, to proclaim the year of the Lord's favor and the day of vengeance of our God, to comfort all who mourn, and provide for those who grieve in Zion—to bestow on them a crown of beauty instead of ashes, the oil of joy instead of mourning, and a garment of praise instead of a spirit of despair. They will be called oaks of righteousness, a planting of the Lord for the display of his splendor. (Isaiah 61:1–3)*

This is the ultimate picture of God's justice: the prisoner goes free. Not because a punishment satisfied the Audit, but because the river restored a mind. To the world, the release of a prisoner is a legal risk; to the Father, it is a biological home-coming. Just like the rebel Barabbas walking free, the least of these are stepping off the stone platform of their crimes and onto the wooden porch of their original design.

I saw this landing strip for the Father's heart in a shared space where the lines between the 'sacred' and the 'secular' had finally blurred. One afternoon, John and I found ourselves in a room where the most polarizing brokenness of the human condition was present—the labels that religion usually uses to justify its gates. On one side was the heavy shadow of a violent past; on the other, the complex, jagged edges of a systemic violation. And there we were—the parents of the violated—standing in the middle of a collision between our history and His Heart.

I won't disguise that our knee-jerk reaction was to close the door of our hearts; the musty courtroom of our past tried to demand a measure of the risk. We wanted to audit the room before we allowed ourselves to breathe. But something inside shifted with a terrifying speed. It was a, *you without sin, cast the first stone* moment. We stood in the holy stillness of that public encounter, tears streaming down our faces, while the Father's perspective overrode our biological alarms.

At that moment, I didn't see offenders or categories. I saw siblings caught in the same weary fog that had once blinded me. As the architecture of my heart was moving, the words of

Isaiah 61 raced through my mind. I didn't just read the promise; I saw the reality. I saw the Year of the Lord's Favor falling like a blanket over everyone in the room—not to ignore the mess, but to restore the mind. It was the first day of a new life —a new wineskin beyond my wildest dreams. I don't have the first clue what I'm doing, but the joy that only the Father can provide is rising like Ezekiel's river, and the water is deep enough to swim in.

16

The Gospel

The Invitation to Sit and Sip

I F THAT RIVER IS DEEP ENOUGH TO SWIM IN, THEN it's deep enough to float. Grab your floaties and a drink —we're going on a float trip, not a rescue mission.

Before you read another word, I want you to inhabit your skin. Feel your buoyancy. Notice how the water—this current of Grace—is doing all the work of holding you up. You aren't treading water, and you aren't trying to reach a shore that's already yours. You are simply in the tube, requiring exactly zero effort from your muscles to stay afloat.

Stop managing the room. Stop auditing your thoughts for bad theology. Just settle into the drift—realize it is just as tangible and secure as your seat at the Triune Table—and pour yourself something to sip. This is your official permission to resign from the Force. You aren't being measured. The Father isn't waiting for you to fix your Ontology before He enjoys you; He is currently, actively enjoying the person in the tube. You aren't a project in progress; you're a Guest of Honor who finally let the current take them.

The Scandal: Haunted by a Corpse

We purchased an anti-gospel of perpetual maintenance. We've been treated as if we are still in Adam, and then we're told to spend our lives trying to act like we're in Christ and be careful to be in the world but not of it. This creates a religious hyper-vigilance where we build moats and fences to keep out the bad guys and the invisible soul ties of our history. We live like spiritual border agents, exhausted by the constant surveillance of our own souls.

What if 'spiritual warfare' isn't a battlefield, but a hallway in an abandoned courthouse? What if the demons we are so terrified of are just the echoes of our own footsteps as we pace the old floors of the audit? We are haunting ourselves with the evidence of a case that was dismissed eons ago, clinging to an Adam-essence—a defunct DNA of distance and deficit—that was buried in a tomb that stayed empty.

The meaty, provocative truth is this: The Dead Don't Need Fences. We have been told to find God, but the reality is that we live and move and have our being in Christ. We aren't trying to get into His presence; we are currently, biologically, and spiritually submerged in it. If you are in Christ, you are not a renovated version of your history; you are a brand-new species. The version of you that was vulnerable to that addiction or trauma didn't just get a fresh coat of paint—he died. You are no longer tethered to a corpse because the Living God now hosts your very being. You aren't fighting a war; you're overcoming a ghost.

To be clear: I am not suggesting that the demonic doesn't exist. There is a very real gauntlet of darkness in this world. But we must understand the physics of the fight: principalities and powers are real, but they require a specific frequency to operate; they require the frequency of Adam.

Our ghost in Adam—that old, defunct essence that believes in distance and deficit—is the part of us that wanders into the gauntlet of darkness. The demonic doesn't just attack you; it attempts to litigate the dead man you used to be. It scans for the Adam-code of shame and performance.

But when you realize your Ontology is a new creation, the demonic loses its landing strip. The dead don't need fences, because there is nothing left for the darkness to latch onto. You don't deny the enemy; you are simply existing in a jurisdiction where he has no citizenship. You don't have to hunt demons when you are currently being hunted by a love that has already swallowed the darkness whole.

The Realized Life: The Evidence of the Gospel

I'VE SEEN THIS REALITY SHIFT LIVES IN A WAY THAT HIERarchical control never could. My friend Keven was lured in on a cold day for a bowl of chili, a hot cup of coffee, and a warm stay. He shared his life freely—a map of multiple strokes and years inundated with meth. He is blind in one eye and carries the weight of decades of drifting.

Keven's life reminds me of the story of the woman at the well. She spent her days hiding in the midday heat to avoid the gaze of a world that knew her shame. But after a chat with Jesus, the very thing that had her hiding was drowned in the Well Himself. She ran into the village not to confess her sins, but to announce her freedom. She ran to tell everyone about the man who told her everything she'd ever done—and yet, for the first time, she wasn't afraid to be known.

Keven has done the same. He has continued to come back to include church on Sundays. His first Sunday, he didn't hear an invitation or an offered prayer of salvation. He heard a rev-elational announcement: "...the lie that God is fickle about you, and would risk you burning in hell for eternity is bull-shit." That morning, he learned he didn't have to do a thing, because God had already moved in and was just waiting for him to notice.

The End of the Bucket List

BEFORE ACKNOWLEDGING CHRIST ON THE INSIDE, KEVEN

had a simple bucket list: he just wanted to know what it felt like to be loved before his life was over. He spent nearly sixty years wondering if he'd ever check that box. Today, Keven tells us he has never felt as loved by people as he does here—and now he knows God loves him, too. The bucket list is gone because the Presence has swallowed the longing up.

Keven doesn't see himself as a recovering project; he sees himself as a missionary. If the doors of the church are open, Keven is there. He alone has led the homeless community in for the peace he found at 'his church'—the place where he was surprised by Love.

Then there's Jesse, a younger guy with his own trail of desperation behind him. One day, Jesse and Keven were talking to me about how loved they feel, but Jesse pushed further. With a twinkle in his eyes, he said, "And now we get to love people in this same way!" as if he had won the lottery.

The Gospel changes everything. It doesn't just settle your debt; it resurrects your heart. Keven cleans the bathroom weekly. Jesse has stepped up to do whatever is needed. They're not earning their place, they simply want to be part of the story. They both have a new lease on life, and it's abundant. These men were an unexpected gift; I didn't know how much I wanted to see the power of transformation that happens under the sheer blessing of the Good News. I knew it for myself after years of playing religious games, and I've known firsthand the truth of a Gospel that settles the score once and for all.

The Compelled Preacher

IN JUST TWO SHORT MONTHS, KEVEN, THE MAN WHO WAS once trying to escape his addiction, is now fantasizing about preaching. His old nature attempts to tell him he's unqualified, and he is scared, but he feels compelled. That is the genuine power of the Gospel. It doesn't just clean up your past; it hijacks your imagination.

What is most staggering to me is what *hasn't* happened: In all our time together, the works of behavior management or character reform has never been exercised. I haven't had to play the architect of Keven's progress, because the Holy Spirit has been doing the renovation from the inside out. We often think we need to spend years excavating for gifting, as if the Gospel were a construction site rather than a birthright. But Keven is the proof that when the Gospel is pure, the reform and fire are automatic.

He didn't wait for Christianity 101 to tell him he was safe; he realized he was already Home. He deleted the old ways he used to soothe his loneliness because he wanted to. He stopped listening to crude comedians because he *chose* to. He didn't need a moat to keep out his past because his past no longer has an owner. Now, he listens to "Mary Did You Know" on repeat—because he didn't know, but now he does.

The Final Boast: The Open Gate

THIS IS THE FINISHED WORK THAT SETTLES THE ETERNAL flames. We often read the end of the story—the book of Revelation—as a looming doom loop of fear. But the real boast of that story is a City where the gates never close.

Restorative justice doesn't just sever a faulty connection; it heals the person so thoroughly that the old hooks of the Adam-essence have nothing left to grab onto. There is no need for a moat when the enemy has been so thoroughly disarmed that he has no citizenship and no power to even knock on the door.

The Settle

TAKE ANOTHER SIP. FEEL THE CURRENT BENEATH YOUR tube. Look at your own crumpled checklist of religious requirements, the shoulds and musts you've been carrying like a heavy legal brief, and watch them catch fire in the eternal flame of the Porch. Listen past the crackle of those burning binders, and you'll hear it: that same, steady whistle from the beginning, no longer distant, but right here in the sun.

Keven's bucket list was for love, and he found it. Your list was for fixing, and it's finished. If Keven and Jesse can stand in the middle of their unedited lives and feel like they've won the lottery, what are you still trying to audit?

The feud is over. The ghosts have no ground to stand on because your being is no longer found in the wreckage of your performance. You aren't a project to be managed, and you certainly aren't a suspect under audit. You are a child of the house taking part in a feast that never runs dry.

Stop running. The audition is over. You are finally Home.

God's not mad.

The distance is a lie.

And you are already holy.

THE ARCHITECTURE OF RECONCILIATION

A guide to the scriptural, linguistic, and historical markers that define the journey from the Courtroom to the Porch.

PART I & II: THE LEGAL DELETION

The Barabbas Paradox & The Kiss of Justice

- **Lestēs (Linguistic):** The Roman term for "Bandit" or "Insurrectionist"—representing the violent, retributive nature of the fallen world that Jesus came to absorb.

- **Lex Talionis (Historical):** The "Eye for an Eye" economy. Jesus's alternative—turning the cheek and offering the cloak—is the active practice of the River, refusing to validate the math of the exchange.

- **The Blindfold of Iustitia (Historical):** The Roman "Lady Justice." Her blindfold represents a justice that is distant and transactional, unlike the proximal, seeing Kindness of the Father.

- **Apekdyomai (Linguistic):** Greek for "To Divest."

The act of rendering the enemy naked and powerless. Christ stripped the "uniform" of the Accuser at the Cross (Colossians 2:15).

- **The Bēma Seat (Historical):** Not a magistrate's bench of fear, but a Victor's Platform. A place of reward and recognition where the "Fire" burns away the facade to reveal the gold of your original design.

PART III: THE ONTOLOGICAL SHIFT

Chapter 8: The Corresponding Strength

- **Ezer Kenegdo (Linguistic):** Hebrew for "Corresponding Strength." One who stands face-to-face to reflect your true nature; a mirror of abundance rather than a filler of lack.

- **Allon Parakletos (Linguistic):** The "Other Helper." The Cruciform Presence who occupies the distance until you realize the distance was a lie. He advocates from your inclusion, not for your acceptance.

- **The Trinitarian Circuit (Theological):**

- **Thelēma (The Will):** The Father as the Origin and the eternal "Yes" toward your life.

- **Enōsis (The Solidarity):** The Son as the fusion point of Divine and Human; our inseparable identity.

- **Parakletos (The Mirror):** The Spirit reflecting the finished fact of Union to our hearts.

- **Koinōnia (The Participation):** The Believer inhabiting the circuit as an occupant, not a spectator.

Chapter 9: The High Cost of Tribalism

- **Limbic Resonance (Biological):** The subconscious way nervous systems "tune" into the internal states of those we recognize as our own.

- **The "DNA Ease" (Ontological):** The shared frequency of Union that eliminates the "biological friction" of the stranger.

- **The Co-Incision (Theological):** The species-level "circumcision made without hands" (Colossians 2:11), where every tribe and tongue was legally "cut into" Christ's death to be "exhaled" into His life.

- **Paschal Exhale (Prophetic):** The single, cosmic breath of the resurrected Christ that reclaimed the human species once and for all.

Chapter 10: Rebirth of the Indivisible

- **Dikaiōsis (Linguistic):** Greek for Justification—representing the act of pronouncing someone righteous and the impartation of a new, restorative life.

- **Hypostatic Union (Theological):** The permanent, indivisible union of Divine and human natures in Christ. It is the guarantee that your unity is based on His Being, not your performance.

- **The Perichoresis (Linguistic):** The "Divine Dance"—the eternal, joyful, reciprocal indwelling of the Trinity that we are invited to inhabit.

Chapter 11: The Freedom of the Tributary

- **The Hired Hand (Archetype):** One who manages a "brand" or "reputation" and must flee when the wolf enters because they have a contract, not a covenant (John 10).

- **The Social Blackout (Mechanical):** The systemic reaction when you drop the "badge" of performance. The room grows cold not because of malice, but because the system has no vocabulary for a child who simply "is."

Chapter 12: The Fruit of Two Trees

- **The Binary Trap (Psychological):** The exhausting architecture of the mind that weighs "Good" against "Bad," unaware that both belong to the same tree of effort.

- **The High Places of the Adjective (Structural):** Using religious titles (e.g., "Strong Biblical Man") as spiritual currency to manage behavior rather than describing a state of being.

PART IV: THE RHYTHM OF RESTORATION

Chapter 14: The Leaking Smile

- **El Shaddai (Linguistic):** From the Hebrew root *shad* (breast). God as the All-Sufficient One, nourishing us from the abundance of His own life.

- **Oxytocin Lock (Biological):** The chemical of attachment that facilitates love-bonding with the Father, quieting the nervous system and replacing the adrenaline of fear-bonding.

Chapter 15: The Mission

- **Mishpat (Linguistic):** Hebrew for Justice—the restorative action of putting things right and bringing the leaning wall back into alignment with the Plumb Line.

- **Relational Eviction (Structural):** The tactical use of isolation or silence to bring someone into compliance; the opposite of the Father's "Non-Withdrawable Love."

ACKNOWLEDGMENTS

This book was born in the dark. It is one thing to talk about the Porch when the sun is shining; it is another thing entirely to find it when you've been ghosted by the very people who share the same table. I've learned that dreams, comparison, and self-protection can be used as a gavel, but a Father is the only one who holds the heart.

Years ago, a young woman spoke a prophecy over me that I am only now beginning to inhabit. She said I was like Humpty-Dumpty—that I would be pushed off the wall and experience brokenness. But she promised I wasn't to worry, because "all the King's horses and all the King's men" would surround me to put me back together again.

I realize now, with tears, that the Kings didn't come with credentials or titles. They came as the unhomed, the outcasts who have a grid for slamming doors. They were the ones God commissioned to stand around my wreckage to put the pieces back together again.

To my Kings—Keven, Alexis, John, Jerry and Kasey, Jasmine,

and Jerry: You guys gave me my face back. You had no expectations, no religious meters to check, and no interest in managing my fire. You didn't want the asset; you just wanted me. Your simple, unedited love was the oxygen I needed. You will always have a home with us.

To John: You held the other end of my heart. When the floor was falling out, your love was steady and unchanging. You've always held space for who I am, even when I didn't fully know. Thank you for being my home.

To our children—Dylan, Elyse, Saydi, Autym, Lilly, and Zayne: You are the greatest exhale of my life. You are my wide-open space, the place where I don't have to be anything but your profoundly proud mama. You are my heart walking around outside of my body.

To Lisa: You have been the steady voice of encouragement and wisdom in a season of noise. Thank you for standing beside me and reminding me of the truth when the narrative of rejection tried to take the lead.

To the Burning Hearts: I see you. If you've been told you're "too much," "too smart," or a "threat" to the status quo—this is for you. If they've used your gift as a reason to lock the door or a dream as an excuse to walk away, I've felt that weight, too. The lid is off. We aren't projects to be managed or problems to be solved. We are alive, we are a provocation, and we aren't going back in the box.

Dear Trinity: Thank you for looking me in the eye when the advisors turned away. You coached me through every Sovereign Impasse until the only sound that mattered was the love in your voice. Thank you for the Grace that caught me when my "DIY" life finally collapsed. You showed me that being "too much" for a system of control is exactly the right amount for a Kingdom of Love.

Finally, to the girl on the gym floor: I did this for you. The second-grader who was waiting for a verdict from people who were never qualified to judge her. The trial is over. The good mask is in the trash. I am home. I am unedited. And I am finally, sovereignly, free.

OTHER WORKS BY ANGIE DAY PETERS

The Rooted Series

- *Rooted Revolution: Embracing the Mess and the Mystery*
- *Rooted Revolution: The Intensive (A Partner Devotional)*

The Awakening Collection

- *Revealed: Awakening You*
- *Rise + Shine: Unlocking Fullness*
- *Ephesians: A Life Transformed*

ABOUT MV PRESS

An imprint of Mavyn Vue, LLC

MV Press is dedicated to the reclamation of the unscripted life. We believe that the most powerful stories aren't the ones that have been polished into a product, but the ones that have been forged in the wreckage and restored by the River. We exist to provide a platform for voices that refuse the "Adjective Leash" and choose to speak from the sovereign ground of their own original design.

For more resources on living unedited, or to explore the vision of Mavyn Vue, visit us at: **http://www.mavynvue.com/**

ANGIE DAY PETERS

Angie is still learning the art of the exhale.

For over twenty years, she has been unlearning the habit of earning her keep. She spent decades navigating the structures of leadership and expectation, only to find that the most profound work happens when you finally stop trying to be the architect of everyone else's peace. She isn't a spiritual strategist or a life manager; she's a fellow traveler who stopped running to see what happens when the dust actually settles.

As the founder of **Unedited Life** and **MV Press**, Angie has traded the polish of religious performance for the honesty of the wreckage. She lives in Junction City, Kansas, where she has discovered that when you stop performing and start showing up exactly as you are, the people who have been ghosted by the world tend to find their way to your door. She believes that while life's most beautiful aspects require the courage to put yourself out there despite the narrative of rejection, they ultimately need permission to emerge.

Her life is a vibrant, unscripted mix of six grown kids, three grandchildren, and her high-school sweetheart, John, who has revealed love to its depths. It is a life that is often messy and rarely follows the script, and she has finally found the beauty in that.

Angie writes from the quiet warmth of a sun-drenched room, offering words to those who are digging for doors that have been unlocked all along. She's probably on the porch right now with a cup of lukewarm coffee, waiting for nothing in particular.

You don't need a map or a resume to find her—you just have to sit down exactly where you are. The restoration is already underway.